Unlearn The Silence

By
Nora Igwe

Table of Contents

Acknowledgments

This book is the voice that rose from a silence I once carried. For that, I owe gratitude to every experience, every question, every moment that made me pause and reflect.

To the Divine Source of wisdom, for whispering truths into my spirit when words failed me, thank you for being the light through every shadowed path.

To my family, your love and quiet strength gave me the courage to unlearn, relearn, and become. Thank you for your unwavering presence.

To the friends who held space for me, in conversation, in stillness, and in truth, you reminded me that healing is not a solo act.

To the teachers and authors whose words guided me when mine were buried, your work mattered more than you'll ever know.

To every reader holding this book in your hands, thank you for choosing to walk this journey with me. May these pages meet you where you are and encourage you to listen, speak, feel, and evolve with grace.

And finally, to the silent parts of me, the ones I used to hide, thank you for waiting patiently. This book is your liberation.

Nora Igwe

Dedication

For the ones who stayed quiet to stay safe. For the ones who performed to be loved.

For the ones who knew the truth but buried it to keep the peace.

This is for you.

May your voice return. May your soul feel seen.

May you remember you were never broken.

Only silenced.

And you, beautiful one, are not silent anymore.

A Message to the Reader

Dear Reader,

This book is not here to teach you something you don't already know.

It is here to help you remember.

To remember the voices, you buried to survive. The questions you stopped asking.

The feelings you pushed away to be accepted.

The truth you knew before the world told you who to be.

Unlearn that silence is not a guide to perfection.

It is an invitation back to presence. To your own voice.

To your own knowing. To your own enoughness.

There is no one way to walk this path.

There is no perfect timeline for healing, for change, or for truth.

Go slowly. Pause often.

Let each chapter meet you where you are.

And when something in these pages stirs something in you:

A memory. A question. A release. A truth, don't rush past it. Stay with it.

That is the moment your silence fades, and your soul begins to return.

With love,

Nora Igwe.

Introduction:

Unlearn the Silence

The call to look within through belief, understanding, fear, change, and truth!

There comes a moment in every life when silence becomes too heavy to carry.

Not the silence of peace, but the silence of pretending. The silence of not knowing how to speak your truth. The silence of beliefs that were never yours. The silence of fear dressed as wisdom.

This book was born in that moment.

It's not a manual. It's not here to fix you. It's an invitation to look inward, to feel what you've buried, and to remember what you may have forgotten about yourself.

We all carry stories. Beliefs, passed down like furniture we never asked for. Understandings, shaped by pain, by joy, by survival. We change, even when we resist it. We fear what we don't understand. And we long for something real, something true beneath all the noise.

Unlearning the silence is like peeling back the layers.

Questioning what you believe, not to destroy it, but to see it clearly.

Listening deeply, not just to others, but to your own inner voice.

Making peace with fear, not by defeating it, but by understanding its message.

Accepting change, not as loss, but as evolution.

Seeking truth, not as a destination, but as a way of being.

Each chapter is a doorway. Not into answers, but into reflection. Not into certainty, but into awareness. As you read, you may feel things stir in you: memories, doubts, hopes, resistance. That's not a problem. That's the beginning of your own voice returning.

We live in a world that teaches us to speak only what's acceptable, to believe what's been handed down, to fear what's unfamiliar, and to ignore what's quietly true. This book is here to help you do the opposite.

To believe for yourself.

To understand more deeply. To change consciously.

To walk with fear instead of hiding from it. And to discover what's been true all along. This is your journey.

Not toward becoming someone new, but toward remembering who you've always been beneath the Silence.

This order mirrors how transformation often unfolds: what we believe, what we fear, what we change, and what we ultimately uncover as truth.

Chapter One:

Belief - The Invisible Architecture

WE ARE BORN INTO STORIES LONG BEFORE WE EVER SPEAK.

Before we choose, we are chosen. Before we believe, we are told. Culture, family, religion, survival, each leaves its fingerprints on our minds, shaping our senses of what's real, right, possible, or dangerous. We don't question it at first; we adapt, accept, and repeat. Until one day, the life we're living feels too small, and we realize the beliefs we carry might not be our own.

Fundamentally, belief is the act of trusting that something is true, even without full proof. But it's more than that.

BELIEF IS ONE OF THE MOST DEFINING FORCES IN HUMAN LIFE. HERE'S HOW I SEE IT FROM A BALANCED PERSPECTIVE

Belief Shapes Reality (to a point):

Beliefs influence how we interpret the world, how we act, and how we relate to others. For example, if you believe you're capable, you're more likely to try, persist, and succeed. This applies to everything from personal growth to relationships and even to healing.

Belief Can Be Empowering or Limiting

Empowering beliefs help people grow, overcome challenges, and find meaning. It's done by believing in yourself, in a higher power, or in the goodness of others.

Limiting beliefs, on the other hand, can trap people in self-doubts like *"I'm not good enough"* or *"Nothing will ever change,"* which can not only hold them back from reaching their goals but can also stop them from even trying.

Beliefs Aren't Always Based on Truth

A belief doesn't have to be true to feel real. People can hold strong beliefs that aren't supported by evidence. This can be both beautiful and dangerous. Belief can lead to acts of love and bravery, or to harm and closed-mindedness.

Belief Can Be a Compass

For many, believing in something provides direction. Be it faith, values, or a personal philosophy, belief gives meaning in times of chaos, suffering, or uncertainty.

Beliefs Can Evolve

What someone believes at eighteen might be totally different at forty, and that's healthy. Questioning beliefs isn't betrayal; it's growth.

My takeaway?

Belief is like fire; it can warm a home or burn it down. Now, how can you shape your beliefs in a way that leads to truth, growth, and positive change?

The key is to be aware of what you believe and why, while being open to growth, evidence, and compassion.

Let's expand on the concept of belief and belief systems from different angles: philosophical, psychological, cultural, and spiritual.

What Is Belief?

A belief is something you accept as true, regardless of whether it actually is. It's a mental conviction, often without proof. Beliefs range from basic assumptions (e.g., "the sun will rise tomorrow") to deep values (e.g., "human life is sacred").

Types of Beliefs

Core Beliefs: Deep-rooted views about yourself, others, and the world (e.g., "I am worthy" or "The world is unsafe").

Cultural Beliefs: Shared norms and values within a group (e.g., beliefs about marriage, family, gender roles).

Religious/Spiritual Beliefs: Ideas about a higher power, creation, purpose, morality, or life after death.

Scientific Beliefs: Conclusions drawn from evidence and observation (e.g., "germs cause disease").

Superstitious or Personal Beliefs: Often based on tradition, intuition, or emotion (e.g., "bad luck comes in threes").

What Is a Belief System?

A belief system is a structured set of beliefs that guide how a person or group sees the world and lives their life.

Examples:

- Religious systems (like Christianity, Islam, and Hinduism)
- Political ideologies (like democracy, socialism)
- Philosophical systems (like Stoicism, existentialism)
- Cultural worldviews (e.g., collectivism vs individualism)
- Scientific paradigms (e.g., evolution, the Big Bang)

Belief systems answer questions like:

What is right and wrong?

Why are we here?

What happens after death?

Who or what has authority?

How Beliefs Are Formed

Beliefs usually come from:

- Family and upbringing
- Culture and society
- Personal experiences
- Education and information
- Religion or spiritual experiences
- Media and storytelling

They can be passed down or chosen, consciously held or unconsciously absorbed.

Why Belief Systems Matter?

Belief systems:

Give people a sense of identity and belonging.

Help interpret life's events (good and bad).

Provide rules or ethics for living.

Offer hope, comfort, or purpose.

Can bring people together or divide them

Can Beliefs Change?

Yes, through:

- New experiences
- Critical thinking
- Trauma or transformation
- Education
- Travel, diversity, or deep reflection

But a change in beliefs can feel unsettling or even threatening. People often resist it, try to prove it wrong, especially if their identity is tied to that belief.

Belief as a Double-Edged Sword

Belief is one of humanity's most powerful tools. It's how we create meaning, love, art, war, science, and social change.

And because it's so powerful, it requires awareness. The healthiest approach to belief is both open-hearted and open-minded, having convictions, but also humility.

Belief as a Survival Tool (Evolutionary Roots)

Cognitive Evolution

As early humans evolved larger, more complex brains, they gained the ability to imagine, remember, and anticipate.

This gave rise to symbolic thought and beliefs, not just about what is, but what could be.

Beliefs helped early humans cooperate in large groups by creating shared ideas of gods, spirits, laws, or ancestors.

Yuval Noah Harari (in Sapiens) argues that shared belief in fictions like religion, nations, or money is what allowed humans to form civilizations.

Cultural Evolution: Belief Systems as Social Glue

Religion, Myths, and Morality

Early belief systems (like animism, polytheism) explained natural events and gave people a sense of control.

They developed into organized religions (Hinduism, Judaism, Buddhism, Christianity, Islam) which:

- United tribes and empires
- Codified laws and ethics (e.g., Ten Commandments, Sharia, Dharma)
- Justified leadership and hierarchy
- Gave people meaning in suffering and death

Belief systems shaped the structure of societies, family roles, gender norms, education, and rituals, all of which are core to human culture.

Belief-Fueled Scientific and Philosophical Inquiry

Ironically, belief also drove the questioning of belief.

Ancient philosophy (Greek, Indian, Chinese) explored what is real, what is good, and what can be known.

Enlightenment thinkers questioned religious dogma and created new belief systems rooted in reason, rights, and empirical evidence.

Science itself is built on certain beliefs:

- The universe is orderly
- Knowledge is discoverable
- Evidence matters

Progress in medicine, technology, and law was often built on replacing old beliefs with better ones.

Dark Side of Belief: Division, Control, and War

While belief can unite, it can also:

- Divide (e.g., us vs. them thinking)
- Justify oppression (e.g., slavery, colonialism, caste systems, etc.)
- Lead to extremism (religious or ideological)
- Spark war (e.g., Crusades, terrorism, or even ideological conflicts)

Belief is powerful, but it can also become dangerous when it is blind or goes unquestioned.

Modern Impacts: Belief in the Information Age

Today, belief is more complex than ever:

Science and faith coexist and sometimes clash.

Social media fuels belief bubbles and misinformation.

People form belief systems not just around religion, but also around politics, identity, climate, conspiracy, AI, etc.

Our challenge today isn't a lack of belief, but too many competing beliefs, some rooted in truth, others not so much.

Evolution of Consciousness and Inner Belief

Beyond organized systems, belief is evolving into more personal, spiritual, and philosophical directions:

Rise of mindfulness, holistic healing, and inner transformation.

Focus on beliefs that foster peace, connection, and compassion.

Less dogma, more inner guidance.

This reflects an evolution of consciousness; a shift from external control to internal awareness.

Positive Impact	Negative Impact
Unites people in a shared identity	Divides us vs them
Drives moral and ethical codes	Justifies control or violence
Fuels creativity, art, and purpose	Can limit curiosity or freedom
Advances cooperation and civilization	Can resist progress and science
Evolves self-awareness and meaning	Leads to confirmation bias and closed-mindedness

Belief is not just a human trait; it's the engine behind our social evolution. It shaped our languages, religions, cultures, governments, sciences, and sense of self. The more humanity learns to hold beliefs responsibly, with openness and reflection, the more we evolve, not just biologically, but consciously.

Beneath religion, culture, or science, let's look at belief as a force in consciousness, identity, and reality itself:

It's a lens through which we interpret reality.

It's a choice, often unconscious, to give meaning to something.

It's a story the mind holds about the world, about others, and about yourself.

You don't just have beliefs; your beliefs shape your perception of life.

Belief and the Mind:

Belief isn't just intellectual. It's emotional, psychological, and even embodied.

You feel your beliefs; that's why they're so hard to change.

Beliefs live in the subconscious like "I'm not enough" or "The world is dangerous."

Even perception is influenced by belief. Our brain automatically filters out what doesn't match our expectations and what does.

Example: Two people can see the same event and interpret it completely differently, just because of what they believe about life, justice, or people.

Belief as a Creative Force

There's a powerful truth in this:

What you believe tends to shape what you experience.

Not magically, but psychologically and behaviorally. This is why belief is central to:

Placebo effect in medicine (you get better because you believe you will).

Confidence and achievement (you take more action if you believe you can).

Relationships (you treat others based on who you believe they are).

Belief can literally become self-fulfilling.

Belief and the Self:

Who Are You Without Your Beliefs?

Here's a profound question philosophers and spiritual seekers often ask:

If you dropped every belief, you hold about yourself, others, God, the world, what's left?

This isn't to say belief is bad, but that it constructs the identity. Many spiritual traditions (like Buddhism or mystic Christianity) invite people to observe their beliefs, rather than be ruled by them.

They suggest:

Peace comes not from the right beliefs, but from freedom from belief attachment.

Awakening means seeing reality without the filters of old stories.

So... Is Belief Truth?

Belief is not the same as truth; it's more like a model or a map. Truth is the territory, while reality is as it actually is. Beliefs help you navigate, but no belief can capture the whole truth.

"The finger pointing at the moon is not the moon." - Nora saying

Beliefs point us toward meaning, but they are not meaning itself.

Belief as Sacred and Mysterious

Despite its limits, belief is sacred. Why?

It's how humans make meaning in a mysterious, uncertain universe.

It's how we reach beyond ourselves, toward love, justice, healing, and the divine.

It's how we choose who we are, even when we don't know for sure.

Your Journey with Belief

If you're still sitting with a belief, maybe ask yourself:

What do I truly believe?

Where did those beliefs come from: experience, fear, love, family, society?

Which beliefs empower me?

Which ones limit or harm me?

Am I open to new beliefs, or no belief at all?

That's a beautifully poetic and insightful way to put it, and honestly, it's profound.

Belief as a plain canvas, and the activities we hold dear become the ink... the painting of our lives, describes belief not just as a static conviction, but as a living surface, something open, receptive, and shaped by our choices, experiences, and values.

Belief as Canvas: An Expanded Reflection

The Canvas (Belief)

It starts blank or nearly blank.

Some of it is inherited (culture, family, childhood experiences).

Some of it we paint ourselves, through curiosity, love, pain, and longing.

The canvas is the foundation of meaning. It doesn't tell the story; it holds the story.

The Ink (Our Dear Activities & Commitments)

The ink is made of our choices, values, and passions.

Every time we act with intention, to love, to create, to question, to heal, we leave a mark.

Even mistakes, regrets, or changes of heart become layers of the painting.

What we care about gives color to what we believe in.

The Painting (Our Life)

The result isn't a fixed image; it's an evolving portrait.

Some parts are bold and clear. Others are messy, abstract, or unfinished.

From a distance, others may see beauty or pain, but only you know what each brushstroke meant.

Our beliefs aren't just in our minds; they show in the way we live, love, forgive, resist, and dream.

Why This View Matters

By seeing belief this way, as dynamic, personal, and creative, you avoid the trap of rigid systems. You treat belief like art:

Intentional but evolving.

Personal but shareable.

Reflective of truth, but never claiming to be the whole truth.

That opens space for:

Growth

Compassion (for others with different "paintings")

Courage to repaint parts when life demands it.

This canvas metaphor reminds us that belief isn't just about what we think is true; it's about what we choose to make meaningful. And that's sacred. You're not just a holder of beliefs; you're a painter of meaning.

You can use these questions to reflect, or even paint, write, or speak them aloud:

If your beliefs were a painting, what colors would dominate the canvas right now?

What "ink" (activities or values) do you keep returning to again and again?

What parts of your painting are still blank, waiting for courage or clarity?

Are there any brushstrokes you want to repaint with new meaning?

No pressure to have perfect answers, just explore.

"The Canvas of Belief"

I began with a silence, a canvas untouched,

A space without borders, no truth to be judged.

Then life poured its ink in the form of my days,

Through joy, through sorrow, through broken and blaze.

My first marks were echoes of voices I knew,

painted in colors of borrowed truths.

But soon I discovered the strokes were my own,

when I dared to question, to wander alone.

I wrote with my laughter, I smudged with my tears,

My love left bold lines, my doubts drew the fears.

Some parts are messy, abstract, and wild.

Others are tender, as the hand of a child.

And though I can't see the whole picture complete,

Each moment I live adds texture beneath.

Belief is not fixed; it's the act of becoming,

The rhythm of breath, the heartbeat still humming.

So, I paint with my truth, and I paint with my grace,

And I honor the canvas.

How does belief shape our inner world?

Belief shapes our inner world more than almost anything else. It acts like the invisible architecture of our thoughts, emotions, self-perception, and even how we process pain or joy.

Belief Shapes Thought Patterns

Your beliefs determine how you think, not just what you think.

If you believe the world is kind, you interpret challenges as learning opportunities.

If you believe people are untrustworthy, your mind looks for signs of betrayal.

If you believe you're not good enough, your thoughts become self-sabotaging.

Beliefs are like filters; they color how your mind processes every experience.

Belief Influences Emotions

Your feelings are deeply connected to what you believe about a situation.

If you believe failure is shameful $\rightarrow$ you feel anxiety, regret, and self-loathing.

If you believe failure is feedback $\rightarrow$ you feel motivation, curiosity, and self-compassion.

The same event can lead to wildly different emotions, depending on your belief about it.

Belief Affects Self-Identity

Beliefs don't just live in your thoughts; they become part of your self-concept:

"I'm not lovable."

"I'm strong, no matter what."

"I always mess things up."

"I have something meaningful to give."

These internal beliefs shape your confidence, choices, relationships, and even body language.

What you believe about yourself becomes the emotional landscape you live in.

Belief Impacts Resilience and Healing

In hard times, belief can be:

A lifeline ("I will get through this.")

Or a trap ("This will never change.")

People who believe they have agency (the power to change their lives) often heal faster, adapt better, and suffer less.

Belief creates a sense of possibility, or its absence.

Belief Can Cage or Liberate the Soul

Some beliefs hold us hostage:

"I'm not allowed to rest."

"I must please everyone."

"I'm broken." Others set us free:

"I am enough, even unfinished."

"Growth takes time and grace."

"I don't need to have all the answers right now."

Your freedom or suffering often depends not on reality itself, but on what you believe about reality.

Belief as a Compass for the Inner World

Beliefs give us a sense of direction: What matters, what to pursue, and what to avoid.

They answer inner questions like: Who am I? What is worth living for? Can I trust life?

They create internal order in the chaos of experience.

Belief in the Inner World

Belief	How It Shows Up
Thoughts	Inner dialogue, mental interpretations
Emotions	Fear, hope, guilt, peace
Identity	Who do you believe you are
Motivation	What do you think is possible or worth trying
Healing	Whether you feel stuck or growing
Inner peace	Whether you feel safe and whole inside

Beliefs can change.

The inner world is not fixed. When you shift your beliefs, especially about yourself, your entire emotional reality can transform.

Inner peace isn't found by changing the world outside, but by becoming aware of the beliefs inside, and learning to choose them with love.

Step-by-Step Inner Belief Reflection

You can write your answers down, say them aloud, or just think through them quietly. Ready?

Identify a Belief You Carry About Yourself

Complete this sentence in your own words:

"Deep down, I believe that I am."

Common examples:

"Not enough"

"Strong, but alone"

"Too much for people"

"Meant for something bigger"

"Not truly loved"

"Always trying to prove myself"

What came to mind for you? (If you're not sure, pick something that feels emotionally charged or that repeats often in your thoughts.)

Where Did This Belief Come From?

Ask:

When did I first start believing this?

Was it something someone said to me?

Was it based on one painful experience? Or many little ones?

Sometimes beliefs come from parents, teachers, culture, religion, or rejection.

How Does This Belief Affect You?

Ask yourself:

How does this belief make me feel emotionally?

How does it influence my relationships?

What does it stop me from doing?

You might notice it leads to overworking, holding back, staying quiet, getting angry, or needing approval.

Is This Belief Still Serving You?

Even limiting beliefs once served a purpose, to protect you, explain something, or help you survive.

But ask:

Is this belief true now? Is it fully true? Do I still want to carry it?

What New Belief Would You Like to Grow Into?

Now imagine you're holding that old belief in one hand, and placing it gently down.

On the other hand, hold a new one, not fake or forced, but gentler, kinder, and more empowering.

Examples:

"I am learning that I am enough."

"I'm allowed to grow without shame."

"I don't have to prove my worth, I just am."

"I am becoming someone I trust."

What belief feels like a seed you'd be willing to plant?

Final Step: Say It to Yourself

Speak your new belief softly, like you would to a younger version of you. Speak it slowly. Let it land.

That's where change begins, not in force, but in tenderness.

Chapter Two:

Understanding

Understanding is not about knowing; it's about beholding. To understand something truly is not just to gather facts or to explain it with logic; that's knowledge. Understanding, on the other hand, goes deeper.

It is when the mind, the heart, and the soul align to meet something, or someone, exactly as they are, without trying to fix, label, or control them.

Moreover, understanding requires Presence, Attention, and Focus. You can never understand anything deeply if you're simply rushing past it.

To understand:

A person → You must listen beyond their words.

A feeling → You must sit with it without running.

A truth → You must let go of your need to be right.

Understanding is a form of humble attention, by carefully processing and connecting what you know into something that truly makes sense.

True Understanding Feels Like This:

The mind says: *"I see the shapes in this picture."*

The heart says: *"I feel the depth in this painting."*

The soul says: *"I embrace the mystery behind this art."*

It's understanding that connects knowledge with purpose. That's why understanding can heal. It allows others to feel and be seen, while helping you to become softer toward life, even in confusion or pain.

Understanding and Judgment

Judgment creates distance: *"That shouldn't be like that."*

Understanding closes the gap: *"I see why it is this way… even if I don't agree."*

This is how compassion is born, not from approval, but from perception without condemnation.

Understanding Is Fluid.

Understanding is not a final destination, only the beginning. It grows as you grow. It shifts as your perspective shifts.

To truly understand is also to say, "I may never fully grasp this… but I will stay open to it."

That openness is what makes us wise, not what we know, but how much we're willing to keep learning, especially from what challenges us.

Understanding is the art of holding truth without needing to hold control.

It's what makes us human.

It's what makes us safe for others.

And it's what allows the world, even its chaos, to become something we can walk through with presence, compassion, and grace.

Understanding Begins with Curiosity, Not Certainty

True understanding starts not with "I already know," but with "I want to know you / this / myself more deeply."

It asks:

What lies beneath the surface?

What pain or story is hidden under this behavior?

What's really being said when words fail?

The moment we drop the urge to define our perspective on things; we open new doors to discoveries.

To Understand Another is a Sacred Act

When you seek to understand someone, you honor their inner world. Not by trying to "fix" them or "win" an argument, you're simply offering space for their truth to exist beside yours.

"Understanding is the other name for love. If you don't understand, you can't love." - Thich Nhat Hanh

This doesn't mean agreement; it means: I see you, I hear you, and your experience matters, even if it's different from mine.

We Crave to Be Understood Most in Our Chaos

Often, we're not looking for answers; we just want someone to sit beside us in our confusion and say: "I can see why you'd feel that way."

When this happens, even our hardest emotions, such as anger, sadness, and fear, all soften.

Understanding not only fixes the pain; it lightens the burden of carrying it alone.

Self-Understanding Is the Hardest Kind

Before you can truly understand others, you must first turn inward. Why? Because you can't have peace with the world until you begin to understand your own inner weather:

Why do I react this way?

Where did that insecurity come from?

What part of me is still wounded?

What do I keep running from?

Self-understanding, as the name suggests, is the bridge between who you've been and who you're becoming.

It sometimes requires brutal honesty, but also deep compassion.

Understanding Is a Spiritual Practice

It slows us down.

It asks us to listen with more than our ears.

It asks us to love with more than emotion.

It connects us with something greater than ourselves, something like the shared human experience.

It's a kind of inner stillness that says:

"I may not have the full picture, but I am open to seeing it."

Why People Resist Understanding

It requires vulnerability.

It means letting go of the need to always be right.

It sometimes leads to seeing the ugly in ourselves or others and choosing compassion anyway.

And every time you choose understanding over judgment, you evolve.

Without understanding, knowledge becomes like a book sealed shut; full of information, but inaccessible in meaning or use.

Here's how it unfolds:

Knowledge Without Understanding is Shallow.

You can memorize facts, repeat theories, or quote texts, but if you don't understand how they connect, why they matter, or when to apply them, it's like collecting puzzle pieces and never assembling the picture.

Knowing is having the map, but it's the understanding through which we navigate the terrain.

Knowledge Without Understanding Can Be Dangerous.

If someone knows how to use a tool or a concept without grasping its purpose or consequences, they might misuse it and cause confusion, harm, or false confidence.

Thus, a person may know how to cut, but without understanding, they won't know what to heal.

Understanding Gives Knowledge Depth, Meaning, and Life.

Understanding transforms data into wisdom by revealing patterns, context, and truth. It lets you not just recite facts, but to live them, apply them, question them, and build upon them.

Knowledge fills the mind; understanding feeds the soul.

So, without understanding, knowledge may inform, but it cannot transform. Through knowledge we can collect all the facts, but understanding is the light that gives shape and substance to what we know, turning it into insight, compassion, and power.

Knowledge is the Seed; Understanding is the Root

Knowledge is what we gather: facts, observations, rules, and experiences. It's the surface.

But understanding is what anchors that knowledge. It connects the dots. It reaches beneath appearances to find why something is true, how it works, and where it leads.

Without understanding, knowledge doesn't grow; it just sits, dry, unrooted.

A person may know the word "love", but until they understand it through loss, patience, or giving, they do not truly know it.

Knowledge Can Be Imitated. Understanding Cannot.

Anyone can copy knowledge. We can Google it, repeat it, or dress it up.

But understanding takes internal work. You have to wrestle with the idea, live with it, sometimes even suffer through it.

Knowledge is external, something we learn or grasp from others, while understanding is internal, shaped by our own interpretation and beliefs about things.

Understanding Makes Knowledge Transformative

Think of knowledge as a spark, and understanding as oxygen. Without oxygen, the spark dies. But with it? The flame will only grow higher.

Furthermore, to truly understand something requires complete openness and willingness. It means, or it's rather essential to set aside your internal ideas and beliefs, just for the sake of understanding. Someone can read sacred texts or scientific theories for years and still miss their meaning, because their heart or mind isn't opened to understand.

HOW UNDERSTANDING IS DEVELOPED

Understanding isn't instant; it unfolds. These are the stages it often takes:

Exposure: Receiving Knowledge

You hear something, read it, or experience it. At this stage, you know of a thing, but you don't yet know it deeply.

Like seeing the ocean from a plane, you've spotted it, but you haven't felt its currents.

Reflection: Sitting with the Knowledge

Here, the mind begins to ask: "Why is this true?" "How does this connect to what I already know?"

You start to see patterns. You wonder.

Like hearing a song and listening again, not just to the melody, but to the meaning between the notes.

Experience: Testing or Living the Knowledge

This is the turning point. Life always gives you the opportunity to live what you know; it could be a moment of love, grief, challenge, or revelation.

You've read about forgiveness, but when someone hurts you, do you understand it enough to act on it? This is experiencing what you know, and that experience makes you understand it.

Integration: When Knowledge Becomes Part of You

Here, understanding moves from your head to your heart. It becomes embodied. You don't just repeat the truth; you carry it.

You no longer have to remember how to be kind; you are kind because you've understood suffering.

HOW UNDERSTANDING SHOWS UP IN DIFFERENT AREAS

- In Love:

Knowledge says: "They love me."

Understanding says: "They show love differently. I must learn their language, not just express mine."

- In Science:

Knowledge says: "Water boils at 100°C."

Understanding says, "Why does it boil? How does pressure affect it? What does that teach us about nature?"

- In Self-Growth:

Knowledge says: "I have trauma."

Understanding says: "This is how that trauma shaped me, and here's how I begin healing."

- In Humanity:

Knowledge says: "We are all connected."

Understanding says: "So when I harm another, I harm myself. Compassion isn't charity, it's the truth."

Understanding is the soul of learning. It is what turns noise into music, facts into wisdom, and existence into meaning.

Deepen to Understanding

Deepening understanding is not just about gaining more knowledge; it's about sinking into meaning, connection, and truth.

Here's a path you can follow:

1. Slow Down and Be Present

Understanding doesn't come in a rush. It reveals itself in stillness, in the moments when you're not just reacting, but observing with attention.

Ask: "What am I really seeing here? What might I be missing by rushing?"

Example: When someone speaks to you, listen not just to the words, but to their tone, silence, emotion, and intent.

2. Ask Better Questions

The quality of your questions will shape the depth of your understanding.

3. Read Between the Lines

Go beyond "What happened?" and ask:

- Why does this matter?
- What is beneath this?
- What does this mean to me and others?
- What are the unseen connections here?

Curiosity is the key that unlocks layers hiding beneath the surface.

Engage with Experience, Not Just Theory

Understanding doesn't deepen in books alone. It needs real-life pain, joy, conflict, and growth.

- Knowledge says: "Fire burns."
- Experience says: "Now I know how it feels."
- Understanding says: "So, I'll handle it with both caution and respect."

Let life teach you. Sit with your experiences. Don't run from them; reflect on them.

Dialogue with Others

Other minds stretch your own. They show you perspectives, blind spots, and truths you can't reach alone.

Thus, speak, ask, debate gently, and listen deeply.

Sometimes understanding comes not from having your idea confirmed, but in having it lovingly challenged.

Be Willing to Not Know

This is big. Humility opens the heart to deeper learning.

"I don't know" is a doorway, a path towards greater understanding, not a dead end. Surrendering what you think you know creates space for what you were not yet ready to understand.

Practice Inner Stillness

Sometimes understanding doesn't come from thinking more, but from thinking less.

Sit in silence, reflect, meditate, journal, and most importantly, ask yourself.

Often, the truth we're seeking is already inside us, but the noise of life drowns it out.

Return Often

Come back to the same idea or experience again and again. Understanding something deepens through layers.

Each time you return, you'll see with different eyes because you have changed.

Like a river, truth looks different depending on the light, the season, and the place you stand.

Understanding is not just something you gain; it's something you become.

The more you open, the more you reflect. The more you live with presence and humility, the more you will carry understanding, not just in your mind, but in your way of being.

Understanding a System: The Heart of Creation

To build anything meaningful, a business, a piece of technology, a story, or even a society, you must first understand the system you're working with.

Because systems are the structures that hold movement, meaning, and purpose.

But what is a "System"?

A system is a set of parts that interact to produce a result. It could be:

- A business (supply chain, customers, finance, delivery).
- A human body (organs, cells, communication).
- A relationship (communication, trust, needs).
- A story (characters, setting, conflict, theme).
- A government, a forest, an app, or even your inner world.

Each system has:

- Inputs (What goes in?)
- Processes (How it transforms?)
- Outputs (What it produces?)
- Feedback loops (How it adjusts?)
- Emergence (Unexpected outcomes from interaction.)

Why Understanding a System is the Foundation of Building It

If you don't understand a system, you might:

- Add parts that break it
- Solve the wrong problems
- Misuse resources
- Build something that looks good but fails in motion

Thus, to build well is to see clearly.

When you understand the purpose, relationships, and limits of a system, you can shape it with wisdom.

Understanding Systems is the Core of Creativity

Many think creativity is just inspiration or imagination. But true creativity is designing something that works, something alive inside a structure. Creativity without understanding is like painting in the dark.

Understanding gives you light, space, and tools.

Understanding Leads to Creative Power Because:

You See the Invisible

You don't just see what it is, you see how it works. You see patterns. Dependencies. Root causes. And this allows you to innovate, not just decorate.

Example: An entrepreneur sees why a city's food delivery system has failed and invents Zipeat (a food delivery app) to solve the need in a creative way.

You Know Where to Intervene

Creativity isn't about changing everything; it's knowing which one change can create the biggest shift.

This is called leverage. And without understanding the system, you can't find it.

You Anticipate Consequences

Understanding lets you see the ripple effects.

What happens if I remove this piece? What will grow if I add this?

Creativity without understanding or evaluating the consequences is just chaos, sometimes uncontrollable and bound to fail.

That's why understanding is important. It turns creative ideas into sustainable innovation.

You Can Break Rules Intelligently

Every great creative mind bends or breaks rules. But not blindly.

- Picasso learned the structure of form before breaking it.
- Einstein studied the classical system before rewriting physics.

Creators first understand, then they re-imagine.

Understanding as a Template

Understanding is a living template, one that shapes how we interact with the world, solve problems, create, and evolve.

It's not a rigid form like a blueprint. It's more like:

- A framework that adjusts to complexity
- A pattern that helps organize chaos
- A guide that helps you know where and how to begin

Why Understanding Works as a Template:

It organizes information. When you understand something, you're no longer overwhelmed by random facts; you start to see structure.

That structure becomes a template for:

- Decision-making
- Planning
- Designing systems
- Teaching others
- Creating new solutions

It Reflects Meaning

Understanding doesn't just say what something is; it reveals why and how it matters.

This gives you a template for insight, to compare, connect, and reflect across different situations.

It Guides Action

Understanding lets you act with clarity.

It becomes a mental and emotional model you can apply in new situations, even in ones you've never faced before.

Like a compass, it may not give you the whole map, but it tells you which direction to start walking.

It Evolves with You

Unlike fixed templates, understanding grows. It adapts as you gather more experience, deeper reflection, or new truths.

So, it's not just a template you use; it's one you grow into.

I could say, "Understanding is not just knowing what's in front of me. It's a template that helps me shape meaning, build systems, create, and grow."

Now, "understanding" and "observing" are two deeply connected concepts, but they serve different roles in how we perceive and engage with the world.

Understanding and Observation

As we have talked about understanding, let's now focus on "observing" and how it differs from understanding.

Observing

- **Definition:** The act of noticing or perceiving something using the senses or attention.
- **Nature:** It can be passive or active, can be just seeing, hearing, feeling, or noticing patterns.
- **Example:** You watch how people react in a conversation, or how a plant bends toward the sunlight.

In simple words, observation is gathering data.

The Importance of Balance in Understanding Holding Space Without Losing Yourself.

Understanding is sacred work. But without balance, it can become a burden.

You begin to overextend. You try to understand everyone and everything, until you no longer understand yourself.

We are taught that understanding means tolerance, silence, or agreement. But real understanding does not mean shrinking; it means seeing clearly, without abandoning your own truth in the process.

Without Balance, Understanding Turns into Over-compensation

You excuse behavior instead of naming harm.

You empathize so much with others that you stop checking in with your own boundaries.

You become so generous with your perspective that you forget to ask:

"But what do I feel? What do I need? What is true for me?"

Understanding without balance is like pouring water into every cup but your own. Eventually, you run dry.

However, balance is what makes understanding sustainable.

You can hold compassion without carrying the weight of someone else's decisions.

You can be curious without abandoning your convictions.

You can listen deeply without staying silent about what hurts you.

Balanced understanding sounds like:

"I see your pain, and I honor mine too."

"I understand your perspective, but I no longer agree."

"I love you, but I'm choosing myself this time."

You are allowed to understand and still walk away. This is one of the most important truths: you can understand someone completely, and still know that they are not meant to stay in your life.

Understanding doesn't always mean reconciliation. Sometimes, it gives the wisdom to say:

"Now that I understand, I know this is not mine to carry."

True understanding doesn't blur your boundaries; it clarifies them.

It doesn't silence your truth; it strengthens it.

And the deeper your understanding becomes, the more essential it becomes to maintain your balance.

Understanding Time and Season

Everything doesn't happen at once, and that's a mercy as it spares us from being overwhelmed. There is a rhythm to life that doesn't rush.

Even when we do rush, there is a time for blooming, and a time for breaking.

A time for letting go, and a time for learning how to hold what stays.

But we often confuse our discomfort with delay, wanting things to happen at once.

We want answers when we're meant to be resting.

We want clarity in the middle of the storm.

We want to be ready before we've been prepared.

Yet time, real time, sacred time, doesn't answer to pressure; it unfolds in seasons, not in seconds.

There's a Reason Seeds Don't Bloom Overnight

You wouldn't pull a flower out of the soil just because you're tired of waiting.

Yet, we do this to ourselves:

- Rushing our healing.
- Demanding purpose in the middle of pain.
- Measuring growth by comparison instead of truth.

What we need to understand is that what if this moment isn't asking you to bloom, but to root?

Every Season Has a Wisdom

The quiet seasons teach you how to listen.

The confusing seasons teach you how to trust.

The painful seasons reveal what you're still carrying.

And the blooming seasons remind you of what was always possible.

You have no control over the season you're in, but you can embrace it, honor it.

You can stop blaming yourself for not being as far in life as you hoped.

You can stop assuming that waiting means failure.

But most importantly, you should trust that time has its own kind of intelligence.

You Are Not Late to Your Life

This is the truth about life that no one says enough.

You are not behind.

You are not too slow, nor are you stuck. You are steeping, slowly, gradually, and continuously.

There are parts of you coming alive in silence. Lessons ripening beneath the surface. Truths forming in the dark that couldn't take root in the light.

Understanding time and season is how you learn to stop forcing and start listening.

You don't have to rush your becoming.

The season will shift. The way will open.

And when it's time, you won't have to chase what's meant for you.

You'll just have to recognize it, because you're finally ready.

Understanding

Definition: The ability to grasp the meaning, reason, or structure behind what is observed.

Nature: Deep, internal, and reflective; it connects dots and gives context.

Example: You realize that sunflowers turn toward the sunlight because of phototropism; they need energy from the sun to grow.

Understanding is making meaning; it's the processing.

The Relationship Between Understanding and Observation

Observation leads to understanding: You can't understand what you haven't noticed.

Understanding sharpens observation: The more you understand, the more subtle things you begin to notice.

Think of observing as the eyes and understanding as the mind.

For example:

Let's say you're trying to build a food delivery system:

Observation: You notice delays happen mostly at lunchtime and near schools.

Understanding: You realize this is due to traffic patterns and school pickups. Now, you can design smarter delivery routes or adjust pricing.

Let's now dive into how to deepen both observation and understanding, especially in ways that fuel creativity, clarity, and better decision-making.

Deepening Observation

Observation isn't just seeing; it's noticing what others miss.

Practices to Enhance Observation:

- **Slow Down:** Rushing dulls your senses. Pause and look again.
- **Engage All Senses:** What do you see, hear, feel, smell, sense intuitively?
- **Ask "What else?":** After you observe something, ask yourself what else might be happening just beneath the surface.
- **Keep a Daily Journal:** Note patterns, behaviors, emotions, and surroundings.

Example:

In a busy restaurant, most people just see "crowd and chaos." However, an observant person might notice:

- Which staff member seems overwhelmed?
- Where customers are hesitating.
- What dishes do people finish first?

Deepening Understanding

Understanding is the meaning you give to your observations.

Practices to Deepen Understanding:

- **Ask Why Repeatedly:** Keep peeling back the layers. "Why is this happening? What's beneath that?"
- **Connect the Dots:** Link current observations with past knowledge or patterns.
- **Challenge Your Assumptions:** Sometimes what we think we understand is a filter, not the truth.

- **Explain It Simply:** If you can explain it clearly, you likely understand it. If not, revisit it.

Example:

You notice delivery drivers quitting quickly.

You dig deeper:

Why? → Long hours, low tips.

Why low tips? → Late deliveries.

Why late? → Traffic + poor app routing.

Now you understand the chain and can act wisely, backed by data.

Why This Matters

When you combine rich observation with clear understanding, you become:

- A better decision-maker.
- A more creative thinker.
- A more empathetic leader.
- A more grounded human.

Try This (Practical Exercise)

The 3x3 Observation & Understanding Drill

Tonight, or tomorrow:

Observe: Pick any situation (at work, home, a store). Note three small details you usually overlook.

Ask why: For each one, ask "why is this like that?" until you reach some insight.

Record it: Write down what you saw and understood. Do this for 5 days.

It trains your mind to see deeply and think clearly. This 3x3 rule builds the foundation of both wisdom and creativity.

Understanding and clarity

These are the two forces that work hand-in-hand, yet each carries its own sacred weight.

Some truths cannot be rushed. They don't come in lightning strikes. They arrive slowly, like dawn. That is the nature of understanding.

We often crave clarity, a quick answer, a straight line, a reason that makes everything make sense. But clarity is not always immediate; it is not found in noise; it is born in stillness.

And understanding?

Understanding is deeper than knowledge. You understand things or situations after you stop resisting and start reflecting. It is the moment when truth stops being something you analyze and becomes something you feel.

You don't understand people by judging them. You understand them by listening beneath the words, by reading beneath the lines.

You don't understand yourself by constantly fixing. You understand yourself by witnessing with honesty, not shame.

And once you start to understand yourself, clarity is the gift that follows. Not before, not during, but after.

Understanding takes you inward, into memory, shadow, silence, contradiction. It slows you down, softens your grip on control, and asks you to see from a wider lens. It says: "Don't jump to explain. Just stay here. Stay long enough to see what's true."

And then, when you are still enough, honest enough, open enough, clarity arrives like light breaking through mist. Not loud, not forceful, but undeniable.

"Understanding is the soil. Clarity is the bloom."

If you chase clarity without understanding, you'll mistake noise for truth. You'll grab at answers without knowing the question. But when you let understanding take root, clarity comes not just with answers, but with peace.

This is not just about intellect. This is about spiritual alignment.

When you understand your season, you don't rush your harvest.

When you understand your story, you stop rewriting it to please others.

When you understand your fear, you stop letting it lead you.

Understanding softens. Clarity sharpens.

Together, they make you whole.

Sit with yourself, not to judge, not to fix, but to understand.

You are not meant to have all the answers at once. You are meant to grow into them.

Let your silence be sacred. Let your confusion be patient.

Let your heart speak when the mind grows tired of its own noise.

Clarity will come, not when you force it, but when you trust yourself enough to wait for it.

I do not rush what is meant to unfold. I trust the pace of understanding.

I open myself to deeper truth.

I welcome clarity, not as control, but as light. I am grounded in awareness.

I am ready to see.

"Clarity is power. The clearer you are about exactly what it is you want, the more your brain knows how to get there." - Tony Robbins

Understanding and Decision

There is a quiet space between what we know and what we choose, and in that space lies the true power of understanding.

Too often, decisions are made in haste, dressed in the urgency of emotion or habit. We react, not because we lack options, but because we haven't yet paused to understand. We choose based on survival, not vision. We repeat patterns because they feel familiar, not because they're right.

And the only way to interrupt this cycle is through understanding. It slows us down. It invites us to look not only at what is happening but why it is happening.

Understanding is not just about gathering information. It is a deep listening to the self. A willingness to see the roots of our desires, our fears, our resistance.

And when we begin to understand, our decisions evolve.

We no longer choose out of fear, but from clarity. We stop needing validation for our choices because we've already consulted something more grounded, our own inner truth. This doesn't mean our decisions will always be easy. But they will be honest. And in that honesty, we reclaim agency.

Understanding does not silence the doubts living in our consciousness, but it helps us live with them. It doesn't remove uncertainty; it teaches us how to move with it. Remember, the point is not to make perfect decisions, but to make conscious ones.

Each time we choose to make decisions through understanding, we rewrite a little part of our story.

And that is how change begins, not from the pressure to decide quickly, but from the courage to understand deeply.

Chapter Three:

Fear

Losing What I Was Never Meant to Keep

There was a time in my life when everything outside looked stable, but something inside me was cracking.

I had built a life around being what others expected. The responsible one. The strong one. The one who didn't ask too many questions. I carried belief systems that weren't truly mine; handed down like family heirlooms. I didn't know I was living in a box until life started pushing at its edges.

That's when the fear came. Not the loud fear of danger. The quiet fear of change.

It came as a whisper:

"What if they don't recognize you anymore?" "What if this new path leads to loneliness?" "Who will you be without this identity?"

And here's the hardest part: I didn't have answers. Only questions. And the uncomfortable truth that the version of me I had outgrown was safer than the unknown truth that was calling me.

But staying the same hurts more than the risk of changing. So, I let go, slowly, not all at once.

I questioned what I believed.

I sat in silence and listened to what my soul had to say.

I allowed some relationships to fade. I made peace with being misunderstood.

It was terrifying.

It felt like death in some moments, like I was losing everything.

But what I lost was only the costume. And what I found, in the depths of my fears, was myself.

Not the polished self.

Not the one that's fit for every role.

But the honest one. The one who could look fear in the eye and say:

"You don't scare me anymore. You shaped me. But you don't owe me.

What Is Fear Really?

Fear is not weakness; it's intelligence misdirected.

It is your body's way of protecting you, and saying, "Wait, this might hurt. This might change something. This might expose something you're not ready to face."

At its core, fear is about loss:

- Loss of control
- Loss of identity
- Loss of love
- Loss of safety

But often, what we fear losing either was already fading or was never truly ours to begin with.

The Two Faces of Fear

There are two kinds of fear, and telling them apart changes everything:

1. **Instinctual Fear:**

This is survival-based. It's ancient.

It protects you from harm like fire, danger, true threats, etc.

It says:

"If you hear a loud growl, run."

"If you see a car speeding toward you, jump out of the way."

"If you smell smoke, look for the fire."

2. **Constructed Fear**

This is story-based.

It grows from the ego, from memory, or from societal pressure.

It says:

"If you speak up, you'll be rejected."

"If you change paths, you'll fail."

"If you rest, you'll fall behind."

This fear is not based in the present; it's a projection, not a prophecy.

Most fears aren't warning you; they are trapping you.

Fear and the Inner Self

Fear often protects the false self, the image we've crafted to be accepted or avoid pain.

But the true self does not fear growth, risk, or truth. It longs for it.

So, when fear arises, ask:

Who in me is afraid? The part that wants to hide, or the part that wants to heal?

A Brief Story: The Fear of Being Seen

There was a time I held back my voice, not because I didn't have something to say, but because I feared being judged for saying it wrong.

Fear told me: Stay small, stay agreeable, stay invisible. But staying safe came at a cost; my soul began to dim.

Eventually, the silence became more painful than the fear.

And when I finally spoke, stumbling, uncertain, yet real, something shifted. Not outside of me, but from the inside.

Fear had not left, but truth had become louder. The goal is not to be free of fear; it is a feeling, you can never be free from it, but to understand if the fear is even real.

Working with Fear, Not Against It

You don't conquer fear by force. You outgrow it through clarity. Try asking:

- What is this fear trying to protect?

- What truth is underneath the fear?
- What would I choose if I trusted myself?

Then choose, not the absence of fear, but the presence of courage.

Fear will knock. Often. But you get to choose:

- Do I answer from the self I've outgrown?
- Or do I respond from the self I'm becoming?

Fear is a gate, not a wall. And you are allowed to walk through it.

Fear is one of the most primal and powerful emotions we experience. At its core, fear is a feeling, a response to perceived danger or threat, something the body and mind use to protect us. But fear is also deeply complex. It doesn't just keep us safe; it can also limit us, shape our choices, or even drive our growth, depending on how we relate to it.

Let's explore fear from a few angles:

1. Fear as a Survival Mechanism

Fear lives in the amygdala. The part of the brain that triggers fight, flight, or freeze.

Without it, we wouldn't survive long, as fear helps us identify and avoid real danger.

But in modern life, most of our fears aren't about physical survival. They're emotional, social, or psychological.

2. Fear in Leadership and Creativity

Leadership: Fear often shows up as self-doubt, fear of failure, or fear of judgment. But being a great leader doesn't mean you try to eliminate fear; it means acknowledging it and acting anyway.

Creativity: Many artists, writers, and innovators fear rejection or not being good enough. But fear can be a signal that you're doing something meaningful. If there's fear, there's also potential.

3.   Fear as a Mirror

Fear can reflect something deeper: our values, wounds, or the parts of us that need healing.

It's a form of inner feedback.

For example:

Fear of abandonment might point to past trauma.

Fear of success might reflect fear of responsibility or change.

4.   Fear as Growth

Every major transformation in life often involves walking through fear.

Change can feel like death to the ego, but also like birth to the soul.

When you walk toward fear consciously, it often becomes fuel, not just a barrier.

Transforming Fear

Observe it instead of reacting automatically.

Name it: "I'm afraid of losing control," or "I'm afraid I'll fail," etc.

Befriend it: Make space for it instead of pushing it away.

Act with courage: Courage is not the absence of fear, but action in spite of it.

Fear: The Shadow That Walks with Us

Fear is often the quiet voice, whispering in our ears, hiding behind our loudest decisions.

It shows up not just when we're in danger, but when we're about to grow; whispering when we speak the truth, when we walk away, when we step forward, or when we say no. Most of us were taught to either fight fear or flee it. But only a few were taught to sit with it, listen to it, understand it, and only then make a decision.

Fear isn't the enemy; it's a messenger. It tells you where you're still attached.

Where you're still unsure.

Where your old self meets the edge of becoming.

But fear also lies.

It tells you, "You can't." "You're not ready." "They'll leave you." "You'll fail."

And if you believe fear blindly, it becomes your God. It builds walls where there could be bridges.

It builds a life that looks safe, but feels small.

The truth is: fear is not the end of the road. It's the beginning of truth.

Because wherever fear lives, something important is asking to be born.

You don't overcome fear by becoming fearless. You overcome fear by becoming more honest.

More present.

More alive than the story that fear is telling.

Here's A Personal Story

I remember a moment when fear didn't just knock; it sat in my chest like a stone.

It wasn't life-threatening. No one had a weapon. I wasn't in a burning building or on the edge of a cliff. But I was about to speak a truth I had never spoken before.

It was to someone I cared about, someone I didn't want to disappoint. I had outgrown a version of myself I'd been holding onto just to stay connected. And now I had to choose: silence or truth.

My hands were cold. My thoughts raced. I rehearsed every way I could say what needed to be said without actually saying it.

I almost walked away. I almost convinced myself, "Maybe it's not worth it. Maybe I'm overreacting. Maybe next time."

But then I paused. I looked inward, not outward.

And in that silence, I heard something simple but strong:

"Fear doesn't mean stop. Sometimes it means this is the edge of change."

So, I spoke. Not perfectly. Not confidently. But honestly.

And when I did, I didn't lose myself. I found a deeper part of me, the part that would rather be real than liked. The part that would rather shake than lie. The part that was growing up.

Nothing dramatic happened. The world didn't collapse. But a version of me that had always backed down... didn't.

That day I didn't run.

And that's the day I started walking with fear, not away from it.

Fear in Leadership:

The Weight of the Crown

Leadership isn't just about guiding others; it's about facing yourself in public.

At its best, leadership is service, vision, and courage. But behind every decision, every direction, every silence... there is often fear.

Fear of being wrong.

Fear of being judged.

Fear of losing respect.

Fear of not being enough.

No one tells you that stepping into leadership means stepping into a mirror that shows your deepest insecurities. Everything about you becomes visible. Your choices. Your flaws. Your limits.

You're asked to move while still searching for who you are.

Many people think leaders are fearless. But the best leaders aren't those who lack fear. They are those who have a relationship with fear, one where fear doesn't sit in the driver's seat.

The leader, who refuses to acknowledge fear, becomes defensive, controlling, or rigid. They confuse control for clarity.

They shout orders instead of listening.

They hide behind authority because they're afraid of being vulnerable.

But the leader who makes peace with fear becomes something different: Grounded. Present. Human. Trustworthy.

That kind of leader doesn't need to have all the answers; they just need to be real. They lead from integrity, not image.

They admit mistakes.

They allow others to shine.

They make decisions from truth, not from the need to appear powerful.

Fear will always walk beside leadership. But it doesn't have to lead.

True leadership doesn't mean being above fear; it means walking through it with clarity, humility, and courage.

Imagine a leader, not as someone standing above others, but as a torchbearer, walking through thick fog. They can't see far ahead. But the people behind them trust their direction, but the leader still has to take each step carefully, uncertain, vulnerable, and exposed.

Fear is the fog.

But courage is the flame.

The flame doesn't remove the fog, but it lights just enough for the next step. That's all a true leader needs, not to see the whole road, but to keep walking with light in hand, even when they're afraid.

"Fear is pain arising from the anticipation of evil." – Aristotle

Fear in Relationship: The Need to Protect What Isn't Safe

Love brings us close. But fear tells us to back away.

In almost every intimate relationship, be it romantic, family, or even friendship, fear hides in different faces: the urge to control everything, the fear of being abandoned, or the distress of being truly seen.

Many of us love from a place of protection. We say what's safe.

We hold back our full truth.

We try to become what others expect of us because we fear that if we show our true selves, they'll walk away.

We confuse silence for peace.

Agreement for love.

Control for safety.

But here's the truth: what fear protects, it also poisons.

The fear of being hurt can lead us to hurt first, by withdrawing, by testing, by staying distant.

The fear of not being enough can make us chase, overgive, or become smaller to feel loved.

The fear of losing someone can make us betray ourselves just to keep them.

We think we're managing the relationship, but often, we're just managing our fear.

Real intimacy begins where fear is acknowledged, not avoided.

When two people can say:

"This scares me."

"I want to be honest, even if it changes things."

"I'm willing to risk being misunderstood in order to be real."

That's where silence breaks. That's where love breathes.

And to face fear in love, ask yourself:

In what ways have I hidden parts of myself to keep someone close?

What truth have I been afraid to speak in love?

Fear in Relationship: When Love Meets the Unspoken

Love asks us to open. However, fear teaches us to guard.

And in between, most of our relationships are shaped, not by what we feel, but by what we're afraid to feel.

Fear shows up when we begin to care.

It might be subtle:

You pause before speaking honestly.

You over-explain to avoid conflict.

You say "I'm fine" when you're unraveling inside.

You choose silence because silence feels safer than rejection.

We don't just fear being left, we fear being seen, because being truly seen means risking the parts of us we were taught to hide.

And so, we become performers in our own relationships, wearing a mask and playing the role we think will keep us loved:

The calm one.

The strong one.

The easy one.

The one who needs nothing.

But love cannot grow where fear is managing the story.

Fear Builds Walls Before We Notice

Sometimes we give too much, not out of love, but out of fear of being forgotten.

Sometimes we shut down, not out of strength, but because we're afraid of what speaking might lead to.

Sometimes we control, because we fear what might happen if we don't.

It's not always obvious.

Fear in relationships often wears the disguise of protection. But protection can also become isolation.

And in trying to save the relationship, we lose ourselves inside it.

Fear Doesn't Always Leave; It Can Loosen

Real intimacy doesn't come from perfection; it comes from presence.

It begins the moment we say:

"This is hard for me to say, but it's true."

"I'm afraid of how you'll react, but I want to be honest."

"I'm learning how to stop hiding in love."

When fear is discussed with love, it softens and turns into an opening for deeper connection, rather than a wall that shuts you off.

It becomes something we walk through together, rather than something we carry alone.

Unlearning the Silence in Love

Unlearning the silence in relationships means:

- Saying what hurts without blaming.
- Naming what you need without shame.
- Letting go of the performance.

Letting someone love the parts of you, once kept hidden from the world.

You don't need to be fearless to love.

You just need to be willing to be real, even when you're afraid.

Because when fear is honored, but not obeyed, love becomes a space where we grow, not shrink.

Choosing Truth Over Comfort: My Personal Story

There was someone I loved deeply. Not just in the romantic sense, but in the way that your life starts to wrap itself around someone else's. They knew my routines, my dreams, my moods.

They made me laugh. Made me feel safe.

But over time, I noticed something subtle inside me: a shrinking.

I stopped saying certain things. I avoided some truths.

I made myself smaller in the places where I was growing, just to keep the closeness from cracking.

I told myself it was love.

But really, it was fear. Fear of disappointing them. Fear of being too much.

Fear that if I changed, the relationship wouldn't survive it.

There was a night I remember clearly. We were sitting in silence, not the peaceful kind. The one that's heavy. The one that fills the room with tense energy when something needs to be said, and both people feel it.

I almost said nothing.

I almost let the silence win.

But then I heard this quiet voice inside me say:

"If you don't speak, you'll disappear."

So, I spoke.

I told the truth, not with blame, not with drama, just with honesty. I said, "I feel like I'm hiding parts of me to keep things okay."

I didn't know what would happen next. I didn't know if they'd get defensive or if they'd walk away. But I knew I couldn't keep living in the version of me that fear had built.

That conversation didn't fix everything, but it changed so much.

Because for the first time, I chose truth over comfort.

I chose my voice over my silence.

And I chose to risk being misunderstood in order to stop abandoning myself.

That moment taught me:

Love isn't about being free from fear.

It's about being afraid, and still choosing to show up as who you really are.

Fear in Career Change: Leaving the Known for the True

We often say we want freedom, but what we really want is certainty.

And nowhere does fear show up the way it does when we're standing at the edge of a career change.

You can feel the pull.

The nudge that says, "This path is no longer yours." But then fear speaks.

"What if you fail?"

"What if you're too late?"

"What if you're making a mistake?"

"What will people think?"

And maybe most haunting of all:

"Who will I be without this role?"

Because jobs aren't just jobs, they're extensions of our identity.

They provide structure, income, status, and more. But when we outgrow them, staying becomes a form of spiritual suffocation.

So, we face a crossroads:

Stay with the familiar pain, and keep the illusion of safety.

Or walk toward the unknown, and let fear be your initiation into growth.

This isn't just about quitting a job.

It's about confronting the beliefs we built our lives on:

- That success looks a certain way.
- That safety is more important than aliveness.
- That dreams must wait until it's too late to dream.

But here's the truth:

The moment we consider change, fear will come. That's not a sign to stop; it's a signal that something real is on the line. Something sacred.

And when your career no longer reflects your truth, staying becomes more dangerous than leaving.

Fear's Real Question: Do You Trust Yourself?

That's what career fear often boils down to, not fear of the world, but fear of your own voice.

Do you trust yourself to start again? To make mistakes?

To succeed in ways that don't look like what others expect?

Do you trust that you can survive discomfort long enough to create meaning?

Because the job you leave behind might give you money. But the work that aligns with your soul will give you a purpose and your life.

The Ability to Start Over

Not a failure, but a return to yourself.

We often treat starting over as something shameful.

As if it means we've failed. As if a new beginning is only for people who messed up the first time.

But starting over is not a weakness. It is not a failure.

It is an act of courage that few ever choose because it means walking away from what's familiar, even if it's no longer true.

Starting over is the moment you stop performing.

It's when the life you've been living can no longer carry your soul.

It's terrifying because you're letting go of a version of yourself that once kept you safe.

You're leaving behind a name, a title, a routine, a comfort zone.

You are shedding the identity that helped you survive, but that now keeps you from being fully alive.

And yes, fear will rise. Fear will say:

"It's too late."

"You've come too far to turn back now."

"What if the next thing isn't better?"

But you must ask fear a harder question:

"What if staying is the slowest way to disappear?"

Starting Over is a Sacred Rebellion

Starting over is not about escaping; it's about returning. It is your way of saying:

"I refuse to live a life that no longer honors who I'm becoming."

It doesn't matter if no one else understands.

It doesn't matter if it doesn't make sense on paper.

What matters is that it feels true, deep in the quiet place where your soul speaks.

You can start over at 30.

You can start over at 60.

You can start over after success, after failure, after heartbreak, after silence.

Every time you begin again with honesty, you come closer to who you really are.

And maybe the ability to start over isn't about chasing something new.

Maybe it's about finally choosing yourself.

Chapter Four:

Change

Change is one of the few constants in life, yet it often feels like the hardest thing to face or embrace.

Let's start with this core idea:

Change is not just something that happens to us; it's something that reveals us.

What Is Change?

At its core, change is:

- A shift in state, direction, or identity.
- A movement from the known to the unknown.
- A process that invites either resistance or renewal.

It can be:

External: New job, loss, relocation, relationship shift.

Internal: Mindset, healing, belief, values, goals.

Why Change Feels Hard

Loss of control: We fear what we can't predict.

Attachment: We hold tightly to familiar patterns, even when they hurt.

Identity threat: Change forces us to ask, "If this changes, who am I now?"

Fear of failure: "What if I can't handle what comes next?"

But here's the deeper truth:

The pain of change often comes not from the change itself, but from our resistance to it.

How to Work with Change (Not Against It)

1. Notice Your Reaction

Do you freeze, avoid, get anxious, overthink, or fight it?

Just naming the reaction gives you space to shift it.

Ask: What Is This Change Asking of Me?

Patience?

Surrender?

Courage?

Letting go?

Change always carries an invitation to grow, only if we're listening.

Big change = small steps.

Ask: What's one simple thing I can do today to move with this change?

2. Reframe the Story

Instead of: "Why is this happening to me?"

Try: "This is happening for me. What might it be shaping in me?"

A Deep View

Change is the soil of transformation. Without change, nothing evolves.

Without change, creativity suffocates.

Without change, you remain a version of yourself that was meant to be temporary.

The Magic Behind Change

Change isn't just movement; it's transformation.

And all real transformation has a kind of sacred, mysterious power behind it.

Change is the Portal

Change breaks the shell of your current self and opens a threshold between:

What was

What is

What can be

That space in between the unknown and the uncertain is where the magic lives. It's where life reshapes you in ways you didn't expect, but somehow needed.

Change Awakens Dormant Potential

Nothing grows in total comfort.

Thus, it's Important to change, so that you can emerge.

It's like a seed in the soil:

The outer shell must crack for the plant to grow.

Darkness must be faced for the light to be found.

Roots must stretch down before anything rises up.

Without the cracking, there's no blooming.

The Fire of Change

Some change feels like fire:

It can come as loss, or in the shape of pain.

Shifting Identity

But even fire holds magic. It doesn't just destroy; it refines.

The person you were is being burned away so the person you were meant to be can rise. Think of it like this:

A caterpillar doesn't become a butterfly. It dissolves into nothing.

Then... something completely new forms from within the chaos.

Change is Life Speaking

When change knocks at your door, it's life whispering:

"You're not meant to stay here. There's more for you, if you're willing to step through."

And that "more" is not always about getting richer, busier, or stronger.

Sometimes it's becoming quieter, deeper, more honest, or more whole.

That's the real magic:

Not just what you gain… but what you reveal within yourself through the journey.

A Soulful Reminder

Change is not the enemy; it is the initiation.

Through change, life teaches you how to let go, how to trust, how to transform… and how to adapt.

CHANGE AS A FORM OF ALCHEMY

What Is Alchemy?

Alchemy was the ancient mystical science of transformation. Its most famous aim: turning base metals into gold.

But real alchemy was never just about gold.

It was about transmuting the self by refining the inner world.

Alchemy = The art of turning suffering into strength, fear into wisdom, endings into beginnings.

Change as Inner Alchemy

Change, especially painful or unexpected change, is the modern version of the alchemical fire.

Just like in alchemy:

The old self is broken down (the lead).

You go through an inner fire (the process).

You emerge as something stronger, truer, and more radiant (the gold).

The 3 Stages of Alchemical Change

Let's break down how every deep change mirror the ancient alchemical process:

1. The Blackening (Dissolution)

This is the dark night, the confusion, the death of what once was.

Your old self, role, belief, or life structure begins to fall apart.

You feel lost or raw.

Magic: This is sacred destruction. It's the womb of change.

Without darkness, the stars cannot be born.

2. Albedo: The Whitening (Cleansing)

After the breakdown, something purifies.

You begin to see more clearly: who you are, what matters, and what no longer belongs.

Grief may still be present, but so is the space.

Magic: This is the return of light.

You are learning how to walk in truth, not illusion.

3. Rubedo: The Reddening (Integration)

The gold begins to emerge.

You no longer seek to go back; you now build forward.

Wisdom, wholeness, and purpose begin to guide your path.

Magic: You become the alchemist yourself, transforming pain into power and fear into creation.

You've made meaning from the mystery.

The Secret Power

The gold was never outside you.

It was always within you. Change simply revealed it.

Alchemy doesn't give you something new. It awakens what you already are, under all the noise and layers.

So, when change breaks you open, ask:

- What am I being purified from?
- What gold is trying to emerge in me?
- What part of my soul is being forged, not just tested?

Simple Alchemical Reflection Ritual

If you're going through a shift now, try this:

Sit quietly. Breathe slowly. Feel whatever is present.

Say to yourself:

"I honor what is ending. I trust what is rising. I allow the fire to purify me."

Ask: "What gold might I discover through this?"

Write one word that represents the you on the other side of this change.

Change is not chaos; it's alchemy.

You are not falling apart; you are being refined. And what's rising in you now… is gold.

Alchemy through change is a sacred way of seeing the world, and it seems to resonate deeply with your inner wisdom.

Change comes not to break you, but to burn away what you are not. It stirs the silence, shakes the soul, and speaks in the language of fire.

Each stage of the inner alchemy holds different wisdom and magic.

1. Nigredo: The Blackening

The end. The breakdown. The unraveling.

This is when everything familiar begins to fall apart. It could be:

- Loss of identity
- Change in relationships

- Career or purpose shift

But deep inner questioning at this stage asks:

- Can you let yourself grieve?
- Can you still be in the dark, without forcing a fix?

Magic in the Nigredo

Darkness doesn't mean death. It means rooting. This is the soil of becoming.

2. Albedo: The Whitening

"Clarity begins to return. The truth begins to rise."

You've released something, even if you didn't want to. Now there's space, quiet, unsettling maybe, but open.

You start to ask:

Who am I without that?

What matters now?

What do I never want to carry again?

This stage asks:

Can you cleanse your thoughts and re-center your truth?

Can you accept that purity sometimes comes through pain?

Magic in the Albedo:

Your clarity is your compass.

What remains after loss is what's real.

3. Rubedo: The Reddening

"Integration. Emergence. The new form."

This is not going back. It's going through.

Here, you've taken the darkness, the lessons, the ashes and now, you are shaping something alive.

You may feel:

Rebirth

Passion

A deeper sense of self, this stage asks:

- What will you create with this new energy?
- How will you live from the truth you uncovered?

Magic in the Rubedo:

You become the alchemist, no longer just changing, but choosing your form.

You Are the Crucible

Remember: The alchemist isn't a magician who escapes change; they are the one who stays in the fire long enough to become something new.

So, wherever you are:

If you're in the dark: Stay with it. Gold forms in shadows.

If you're in the quiet: Listen. Truth returns in stillness.

If you're in the rising: Move with purpose. You've earned your wings.

Change as Evolution

A Perspective on Growth and Becoming

Change is often seen as disruption, uncertainty, or loss of the familiar. But if we look deeper, change is not just an event; it is evolution in motion.

Change Is the Pulse of Life

Every living thing evolves, cells divide, stars collapse and form, minds stretch and reshape. In that same rhythm, every change we experience is life's way of adapting, refining, and realigning us with what's next.

Nothing in nature resists change, trees shed leaves, animals migrate, rivers reroute.

Resistance belongs more to fear than to truth.

Evolution Is Not Always Loud

Evolution doesn't always roar. Sometimes it whispers:

A new idea that won't leave your mind.

A loss that teaches you to value differently.

A quiet decision to let go.

These small changes accumulate into a larger transformation, leading to the evolution of your character, awareness, and purpose.

Pain as Part of Evolution

Like the molting of a shell or the breaking of a cocoon, change can hurt. But the pain is not punishment; it's pressure that births growth.

Without discomfort, evolution has no fuel.

The discomfort you feel in change is the cracking of what no longer fits.

From Reaction to Conscious Evolution

We often react to change. But when we recognize it as evolution, we participate in it consciously.

Instead of asking "Why me?" we begin to ask "What is this shaping me into?"

Instead of fearing the unknown, we become curious explorers of the next version of ourselves.

You Are Not Static

You are not meant to stay the same. Your values, thoughts, desires, and even your wounds evolve. And when they evolve, let them.

Change is not the opposite of stability; it is how deeper stability is born: rooted in who you are becoming, not who you were.

Change as Evolution

Change as evolution applies to leadership, relationships, and creativity, each one being a dynamic space where transformation is the most critical element for growth.

Leadership

- Old View:

Leadership is often mistaken for maintaining control, consistency, or preserving systems.

- Evolved View:

True leadership is guiding through change, not guarding against it.

The best leaders don't resist evolution; they read it, respond to it, and sometimes initiate it before others even see it coming.

Why? Because they understand:

People change, so leadership must adapt.

Markets shift, so vision must stretch.

Crises come, so courage must grow.

A stagnant leader leads a sinking ship. But an evolving leader builds a ship that learns to sail through storms.

Thus, embrace change not as failure, but as refinement. The leader evolves first, so others, guided by them, can evolve safely.

Relationships: Growth or Ghost

- Old View:

Relationships are meant to be constant, where people can meet, bond, and remain the same over time.

- Evolved View:

Healthy relationships are living ecosystems. If you don't allow space for evolution, they suffocate.

People change dreams.

They heal or develop new wounds.

They outgrow versions of themselves.

But the question is: Can both parties evolve together?

Relationships fail not always because of a lack of love, but because one or both refuse to grow into who they're becoming.

Love is not about holding onto someone's past self. It's about being willing to re-meet and re-know them in every new chapter.

Creativity: Reinvention or Repetition

- Old View:

Creativity is about mastering a style or skill and repeating success.

- Evolved View:

Creativity is a change-seeking form. If you create without evolving, your work becomes a museum of past relevance, offering nothing more than outdated ideas.

Creative evolution means:

Leaving behind what "worked" to explore what wants to emerge.

Listening deeply to inspiration, not just productivity.

Allowing yourself to create badly, awkwardly, freely because that's where new genius hides.

Creativity without evolution is imitation. Creativity with evolution is innovation.

Ask not "Is it good?" but "Is it true to where I am now?" Authentic creativity evolves you as much as the work.

In all three, leadership, relationships, and creativity, we face a choice:

Cling to "What Was", or evolve into "What Can Be."

Change isn't just happening to you. It's happening through you.

Impact of change as evolution in

1. Leadership

Leadership is not preserving the known; it's stewarding the unknown.

Change tests leaders, but evolution defines them.

When a leader evolves, they invite their team to grow beyond roles and routines. But when a leader resists change, they become outdated while the world moves forward.

An evolved leader:

- Listens more than lectures.
- Learns in public.

- Admits what no longer works.
- Models' flexibility, not perfection.

Evolution in leadership is less about hierarchy, more about humility.

It's not about having the answers; it's about creating space where better answers can emerge.

A leader stuck in the past delays the future.

Relationships

Relationships either evolve or dissolve.

We often want people to stay the same because it feels safer. But true connection grows when we allow one another to change and not suffocate.

Evolved relationships make space for reinvention, for emotional and spiritual shifts. In contrast, unevolved relationships punish change, holding partners hostage to who they once were.

For you, letting someone evolve doesn't mean losing them; it means learning them again.

Letting yourself evolve doesn't mean betrayal; it means honoring truth.

Love that evolves says: *"I'm committed to who you are becoming, not only to who you were when first met."*

Creativity

Creativity thrives in evolution. Staying still kills the current.

Creativity as evolution means:

- Daring to move past your own expectations.
- Risking rejection to find revelation.
- Allowing your voice, style, or process to shift, even if it means unlearning what made you "good."

If you're not evolving in your creativity, you're not creating, you're simply repeating what you've already created.

The creative spirit is a living thing. It wants to become, not just perform.

Change is not a break. It's becoming.

In leadership, in love, in expression, change is the motion that matures us.

To resist change is to resist growth, but to evolve through change is to live fully.

Change as Karma

Every Shift as a Mirror of Motion

To see change as karma is to recognize that change is not random; it is a return of your past choices and behaviors.

It is life's way of responding to what has been set in motion by us, through us, and sometimes before us.

What Is Karma, Truly?

Karma is not punishment. It's not instant revenge or divine wrath.

Karma is cause and effect.

It's energy responding to energy. It's a motion meeting its consequence.

So, when change comes into our lives, unexpected, disruptive, or even beautiful, it may be:

- The return of our intentions.
- The echo of forgotten choices.
- The balancing of patterns we inherited or created.

Karma is not the universe judging you. It's the universe reflecting on you.

Change as a Reflection, Not a Reaction

When we begin to see change as karmic, we move from being the victim to a witness.

That betrayal? A mirror of where trust was ignored, either toward others or yourself.

That sudden breakthrough? The flowering of seeds planted long ago in silence.

That repeated struggle? A cycle asking to be completed. Not punished, but understood.

Every change is an invitation to become more conscious of your past actions, patterns, and beliefs.

Karma Is Not Just Past: It's Now

Karma is often misunderstood as past-bound. But karma is also:

- This moment's choice.
- Your current mindset.
- What you sow with your reactions to change.

If you meet change with bitterness, you deepen resistance. However, if you meet change with awareness, you plant liberation.

How you respond to change creates karma just as much as what caused it.

Change as Karma in Practice

Ask: What might this change be returning to me? Not as blame, but as understanding.

Observe patterns: Are similar types of change repeating? What lesson remains unintegrated?

Honor cycles: Karma doesn't just punish; it also heals. Some change ends cycles you never knew were closing.

Create new karma now:

- Respond to change with presence.
- Choose clarity over fear.
- Let the new energy you generate rewrite the future.

Change is the movement caused by karma.

And karma is not here to haunt you; it's here to evolve you.

When you stop fearing change and start listening to it, you stop repeating karma and start liberating it.

Becoming the Change

We often ask, "Why is this happening to me?"

But in these moments of stillness, a deeper question arises: What is this returning to me?

To see change as karma is to see life, not as random chaos, but as a delicate response system. Every shift, every ending, every unexpected path might be an echo of something we've put into motion: A thought. A fear. A choice. A silence.

Karma is not punishment; It is the intelligence of cause and effect.

Not in the narrow sense of morality, but in the wide sense of energy: You emit, and life replies.

So, when change appears at your doorstep, it may not be a stranger.

eIt might be the return of something familiar, something forgotten, something unresolved.

Examples of Change as Karma:

A relationship collapses, not because of sudden incompatibility, but because years of avoidance finally surfaced.

A new opportunity opens, not from luck, but from an old act of courage that quietly shifted your future.

A pattern repeats until you notice it, break it, or surrender to what it's asking of you.

This karmic lens is not meant to inspire guilt, but curiosity. It brings power back into your hands.

Because karma is not just what was; it's what is becoming. Every time you respond to change with:

- Awareness instead of reaction
- Softness instead of control
- Courage instead of resistance

…you interrupt karmic cycles and birth new ones.

The way you meet change becomes your new karma.

So, ask yourself:

What patterns are returning?

What stories want to end?

What energies are asking for release?

In this way, karma becomes a compass, not a curse. And change becomes the messenger, not the enemy.

The Fear of Change and the Illusion of Control

We don't fear change because we are weak. We fear change because we confuse certainty with safety.

The mind clings to patterns, what it knows, what it can predict, and what it has survived before. Even if those patterns are painful, they are familiar.

And to the unconscious mind, familiar pain feels safer than unfamiliar freedom.

The Illusion of Control

Control is the armor we wear to protect us from change. But it is made of glass.

One loss, one betrayal, one unexpected shift, and it shatters.

We try to control:

People, so we feel secure.

Outcomes, so we feel powerful.

Timing, so we feel ready.

But life does not ask for control. Life asks for participation.

And participation requires presence, not prediction.

Control is rooted in fear, while presence is rooted in trust.

Why We Fear Change

Change threatens the identity we've built.

It constantly whispers that, "If everything shifts, who will we be?"

This fear runs deep:

- The fear of being unprepared.
- The fear of not being enough.
- The fear of losing what made us feel valuable.

But this is a false fear.

Because who you truly are cannot be lost in change; only revealed.

What dissolves in change is not the real you, but the parts of you that can no longer survive in truth.

Trusting the Current

When we resist change, we often feel stuck or exhausted. But when we flow with it, something ancient awakens:

- A deeper intelligence.
- A quieter confidence.
- A natural rhythm.

This is not passive surrender.

It is co-creation; a conscious willingness to move with life's deeper tide.

The soul does not fear change. The soul is change.

There was a season in my life when everything I thought was secure began to unravel.

The job I had worked years to secure was suddenly gone due to company cutbacks, they said. The relationship I had poured my heart into ended with quiet finality. And just weeks later, a close friend I had leaned on emotionally moved away, without much warning.

It felt like the floor had been pulled from beneath me.

At first, I tried to hold everything together. I updated résumés, masked my pain with productivity, and told myself I just needed to "stay positive."

But inside, I was crumbling.

I remember lying awake one night, overwhelmed and afraid, thinking:

"If I'm not the one with the job, the relationship, the plan, then who am I?"

What I didn't realize then was that I wasn't falling apart. I was simply falling out of who I thought I had to be.

What ended wasn't my life.

What ended was the illusion of control I had clung to so tightly.

In the space that opened, something new began to take root.

I started listening to myself, not just my expectations.

I slowed down. I stopped trying to prove anything.

I painted and wrote more. I noticed what made me feel alive again, not impressive, but real.

That season didn't break me; it unmasked me.

It showed me that what I was afraid of losing had become a cage.

And change, as terrifying as it was, became my doorway back to presence.

Sometimes, life will take everything you think you need, just to show you what's truly yours.

Awakening Through Change

Not all awakenings come wrapped in beauty.

Some arrive as endings, breakdowns, or silence where connection used to be.

But every genuine awakening begins the same way: Something within us can no longer stay asleep.

Change, especially unwanted change, is often the alarm.

When Life Disrupts, It Reveals

Awakening doesn't always look like bliss. Sometimes it looks like:

- The moment you realize you've been living someone else's dream.
- The quiet after heartbreak, where you finally hear your own voice.
- The emptiness that demands truth over performance.

Change removes what numbed us.

What's left is raw. But it's real.

The Inner Unraveling

Awakening isn't about becoming someone new.

It's about remembering who you've always been, but were too afraid or distracted to embody.

That memory returns as change:

- A death forces you to confront what matters.
- A relocation cracks open new dimensions of self.
- A loss reveals what was already gone long before it ended.

We often say, "This changed me." But truthfully?

It woke up the part of you that was ready all along.

Awakening Is Not Always Loud

It doesn't need a mountaintop or a dramatic moment. Sometimes it whispers:

"You're not meant to stay here."

"You're worth more than what you're settling for."

"It's time."

You won't always feel ready.

But awakening doesn't ask for readiness; it asks for honesty.

A Gentle Moment of Awakening

There was a day, months after my life had unraveled, when I sat alone in a café, not doing, not fixing, just being. A quiet rain tapped the windows. I had no job, no plan, no clear label to wear that day.

And for the first time, I didn't feel like I had to be anything other than alive.

I wasn't successful by the world's standards, but something inside me whispered:

"This is peace. And it's real."

That moment didn't look like much from the outside. But inside, something sacred shifted.

Awakening rarely begins with fireworks.

It begins when the noise fades enough for you to hear yourself again.

Surrender as Power

We are taught that surrender means giving up.

That it is the language of weakness, of loss, of defeat.

But in truth, surrender is not the end of strength; it is the beginning of a deeper kind.

One that doesn't rely on control, image, or resistance.

One that moves with life, not against it.

Surrender is not passive.

It is the most active trust you can embody.

Control and Flow

We grip so tightly:

- To what we think we should be.
- To the version of our life we imagined.
- To outcomes that give us identity.

But change will come. And when it does, what you resist will persist, and what you try to force will fracture.

Surrender is not saying, "I don't care." It is saying:

"I will meet this moment as it is, not as I wish it were."

That's where the real power lives.

Picture a river. If you fight it, you exhaust yourself.

But if you surrender to its currents, not carelessly, but attentively, you move with grace, even through unknown waters.

Surrender is alignment. It's:

- Saying yes to the timing you don't understand.
- Letting go of answers that haven't arrived.
- Trusting that clarity often comes after release, not before.

Surrender doesn't shrink you. It frees you to become something wider than your fear.

I once held onto a version of myself that felt "successful." A job title, a routine, an image that made others proud.

But I was exhausted. Quietly disconnected. And yet, I was afraid to let go.

I told myself it was "security." But really, it was a disguise.

The day I surrendered, I had no guarantee of what came next. But I had found peace within myself.

Not relief, but a stillness I hadn't felt in years. And in that stillness, a new space opened:

- For truth.
- For creative freedom.
- For deeper love.

None of that could enter while I was busy pretending.

The Secret of Surrender

Surrender isn't about losing power.

It's about realizing that you are not the source of power; life is.

When you release your grip, you don't fall; you finally flow.

Your hands were full of the past.

You had to let go before you could carry what was meant for you.

Creating Through Conscious Change

Change doesn't just happen to you.

At a deeper level, you are co-creating it.

When you awaken through change, when you surrender with intention, something profound becomes possible:

You begin to create with life, not just survive it.

From Reaction to Creation

Most people live in reaction mode:

A change happens → they scramble.

A loss occurs → they numb.

A shift appears → they resist.

But conscious change asks something different: What will you make with this?

To create through change means:

- Choosing meaning instead of defaulting to despair.
- Turning wounds into wisdom.
- Letting breakdowns become the blueprint for breakthroughs.

Conscious change is not about control.

It is about participation, with presence, clarity, and courage.

Change as a Creative Force

Every artist, healer, thinker, or builder has met change and used it as fire:

- Toni Morrison wrote after loss.
- Maya Angelou spoke truth after trauma.

Creators, across time, shaped beauty from chaos.

The same force that tears down can also be used to rebuild: wiser, cleaner, freer.

Ask yourself:

What is this change trying to teach me to create?

What wants to emerge through me now that the old has fallen away?

What can I make of this moment that future me will thank me for?

Creating from the Inside Out

When you create through conscious change, it's no longer about proving or performing. It's about expression rooted in alignment.

You build:

- A life that reflects your truth, not your fears.
- A voice that speaks what matters, not what pleases.
- A path that feeds your soul, not just your image.

Creation through change is not loud. It is honest.

The Day I Created Forward

After fear and surrender came something unexpected: inspiration.

Not in the grand, world-changing sense, but in the quiet sense of possibility.

I picked up my journal and wrote one sentence: "Maybe this falling apart is a kind of design."

From that line came pages.

From those pages came vision.

From vision came new choices: small, clear, aligned.

I wasn't just reacting anymore; I was responding with creativity.

And in that response, I was no longer a victim of change; I was an author within it.

To create through change is to become a mirror of life itself, always shifting, always rising, and always becoming something more whole.

Becoming the Change

In the end, we come to realize:

Change is not a threat; it is the invitation.

It is the space between versions of ourselves.

It is the mirror that doesn't just reflect, but reveals.

We begin by fearing change. Then we learn to survive it. Eventually, we learn to trust it.

And if we stay open long enough, we become it.

You Are the Living Change

You are not separate from the shifts around you. You are not a fixed self being tossed by storms. You are:

The ending and the new beginning.

The one who fell apart and the one who rose after.

You are not just in charge; you are made of change.

The most conscious life is not the most controlled one.

It is the one most aligned with what is real, present, and unfolding.

From Reflection to Transformation

This is your moment to pause and ask:

- What change am I resisting and why?
- What would it feel like to meet it with awareness instead of fear?
- What part of me is being asked to evolve?
- What am I now being called to create?

The old way taught you to fear endings, but the conscious way shows you that endings are the soil of becoming.

Surrender doesn't make you weak; it's a path that connects you with life's intelligence.

Awakening isn't rare; it's what happens when you finally tell the truth.

And karma isn't punishment; it's the wisdom of motion returning.

To become the change is to live fully awake, no longer clinging, no longer hiding, no longer waiting.

The Power of Intention

Intention is the soul's whisper before action. It is the unseen thread that weaves purpose into motion.

Most people act without asking why. They move, speak, build, and destroy, all without ever pausing to examine the origin of their momentum. But intention is where true transformation begins. It is the seed before the bloom, the breath before the word, the thought before the shape of reality.

To live with intention is to live consciously. It is the bridge between awareness and choice, and between belief and manifestation.

Without intention, we drift. With it, we direct.

Intention vs. Habit

Many confuse habits for intentions. But habits run on automation that are formed by repetition, not reflection. Intention, on the other hand, requires us to be present. It demands we check in with ourselves.

Ask:

- Why am I doing this?
- What energy is fueling my actions, fear, love, ego, or alignment?

- What do I want to create, and who do I become in the process?

When you strip away the noise, intention becomes your mirror. It shows you what you're really chasing and why.

The Energy of Intention

Intention is not just a decision; it's an energy. What you carry within silently influences what you attract, how you react, and the direction your life takes.

Set intention in fear, and you will build success that feels hollow. Set it in truth, and even failure becomes a form of growth.

There is power in stating your intention aloud.

There is courage in writing it down.

There is magic in embodying it daily.

Living with Intention

To live with intention does not mean having everything figured out. It means returning, again and again, to your center. It means balancing your actions with your inner compass, and doing so imperfectly.

Practice this:

Start your day with a small intention. Not a task, but a tone.

"Today, I choose to be gentle with myself."

"Today, I move with clarity and courage."

Notice when you're drifting and bring yourself back, not to control, but to realign.

Intention and Change

Every meaningful change begins with intention. Healing, leaving, growing, or creating, intention opens the door for all. It is not a guarantee of outcome, but a declaration of direction.

When your intention is clear, even chaos becomes purposeful, even endings feel like beginnings. So, ask yourself often:

What am I intending with this thought? This word? This silence?

And let that awareness lead you home.

"My mission in life is not merely to survive, but to thrive; and to do so with some passion, some compassion, some humor, and some style." - Maya Angelou

Maya Angelou is speaking about choosing how to live, not just existing, but doing so on purpose. That's the heart of intention.

"Not merely to survive..." implies that life can be lived unconsciously, just getting by.

"...but to thrive..." is a declaration of intention: I choose to live fully.

The words passion, compassion, humor, and style are not just outcomes; they're intentional energies she brings into her life. She's not leaving them to chance.

Her life, as described in the quote, is an example of living with deliberate energy, rather than just following a routine.

Intention and Action are two essential forces in personal growth, creativity, and meaningful change. Though they are deeply connected, they serve distinct roles. Here's a breakdown that may be helpful for your writing or reflection:

1. Intention Definition:

Intention is the inner aim, the purpose or reason behind what we do. It's the seed, the silent whisper that shapes our focus and energy before anything visible happens.

Qualities of Intention:

- Rooted in the inner world.
- Often abstract or emotional.
- Affects direction, clarity, and alignment.
- Sets the tone for action (loving, fearful, courageous, etc.).

Examples:

- *"I want to heal."*
- *"I intend to listen more deeply."*
- *"I choose to create from love, not fear."*

2. Action

Definition:

Action is the outward expression of intention. It's how we move, speak, and engage with the world. Without action, intention stays dormant.

Qualities of Action:

- Tangible and observable.
- Brings intention into reality.
- Requires courage, discipline, or choice.
- May not always align with the original intention if they are carried out without awareness.

Examples:

- Attending therapy sessions
- Calling a friend to apologize
- Launching a new idea

Their Relationship

Intention without action is a dream not lived. Just as action without intention can be aimless or hollow.

However, when intention and action align, you create integrity, a powerful state where what you believe and what you do are in harmony.

To begin that self-inquiry, ask yourself:

"What is the hidden intention behind my daily actions? And do my actions reflect what I truly value?"

Chapter Five:

Truth

There was a season in my life when everything looked like it was working. Only I wasn't.

I had the structure. I had the title. I had the respect of others. But every day felt like a performance.

Every day I woke up with a tightness in my chest that I called 'routine,' but in reality it was dread filling me.

I kept telling myself, "You should be grateful."

I kept reminding myself how hard I worked to build this life.

But gratitude without truth is a prison with nice wallpaper.

One evening, I found myself alone in a quiet room. I don't remember what triggered it. Maybe it was just the weight of silence. Maybe it was the sound of my own breath and the realization that I'd been holding it for too long.

And then something broke inside of me. Not in the angry, chaotic way, but in the quiet, sacred way.

The kind of breaking that comes when your soul whispers, "It's time."

I didn't have a plan.

I didn't know what I'd do next.

But I knew this: I could no longer pretend.

So, I let it fall.

The job. The identity. The version of myself that had held me together but was now holding me back.

It wasn't easy. It wasn't glamorous. But it was real.

And that moment, when I chose truth over stability, that was the moment I came home to myself.

Truth doesn't arrive with applause.

It doesn't care about your reputation or your résumé. It isn't always convenient. It doesn't always feel good. But it is always clean.

Unlike belief, which we inherit and repeat, truth is something we meet.

It doesn't shout. It doesn't explain. It simply stands.

We spend years, sometimes lifetimes, avoiding our own truth because it threatens the life we built around fear.

But when truth finally arrives, it doesn't come to destroy you.

It comes to free you.

And often, that freedom costs everything you built in silence.

Truth doesn't always give comfort. But it always gives clarity.

And in that clarity, even your pain becomes meaningful.

Because the moment you live your truth, no matter how small, you are no longer asleep in your own life.

What Is Truth?

Truth is not a fact. It is not an opinion.

It is not a perfect sentence, or a fixed rule.

It's not even always something you can explain.

Truth is a feeling of alignment.

A moment when your inner and outer world stop fighting.

A quiet knowing that doesn't shout, but doesn't shake either.

It's what remains when the performance ends.

What rises when fear steps aside.

What lives in you when no one is looking, and when nothing needs to be said.

Truth is Not Inherited

We're taught many things and told that they are true.

But the real truth is never just handed down; it must be realized.

It's not about rejecting everything you've learned. It's about asking: *"Do I still feel whole when I stand beside this belief?"*

"Does this still resonate when I am quiet and alone with it?"

Truth that belongs to you, from your heart, from your experience, has a different feeling. It feels clean, solid, something that's not forced, but natural.

It doesn't beg for approval.

Truth is Not Always Comfortable, But It's Always Clear.

Sometimes, truth costs you the life you've built around avoiding it.

It may ask you to leave the job, the relationship, the identity.

It may ask you to outgrow a version of yourself that once kept you safe.

Truth doesn't always feel good at first.

But it always feels right underneath the discomfort.

And eventually, it brings peace, not because everything is easy, but because you are no longer divided inside.

Truth is Not Just Something You Speak; It's Something You Live.

The real truth shows up in:

- What you can no longer pretend to believe.
- The conversations you stop having.
- The places you stop forcing yourself to fit.
- The joy you begin to feel when you are finally honest.
- Sometimes truth speaks.

Sometimes, it walks away. Other times, it says nothing, but leaves the door open behind it.

So, What Is Truth?

Truth is the quiet place inside you that never needed permission.

It was always there, beneath all the noise, the fear, the silence.

You don't have to go find it.

You just have to stop running from it.

And once you stop running, you realize it was never chasing you; it was waiting for you to come to it.

Relationship between Truth and Love

When Being Real Risks Being Alone

We are told that love is everything.

That to be loved is to be whole.

That if we just love enough, things will work. But here's the part no one tells you:

Sometimes, the truest thing you can do will cost you the thing you love most.

Sometimes, love asks for peace. But truth asks for disruption.

Sometimes, love wants comfort. But truth demands clarity.

We want to believe that they will always walk hand in hand.

But sometimes, truth and love go in different directions. And you have to choose:

Do I stay in love with them, or do I stay honest with myself?

The Love That Requires Silence Is Not Love

If staying in love means hiding your truth, if it means biting your tongue until it bleeds, if it means shrinking, suppressing, filtering, then it isn't love, it's an attachment, it's fear, it's performance, but not love.

Real love doesn't fear your truth.

It might not always understand it.

It might not always want it.

But it will not punish you for speaking it.

And yet, telling the truth might still cost you the relationship. That's the part no one wants to face.

But here's something more sacred than being loved:

Being real.

The Love That Stays After the Truth Is Spoken, That's the Love You Can Trust.

There is a love that survives truth.

A love that bends, but doesn't break.

A love that listens, even when it's uncomfortable.

That adapts, grows, pauses, and returns.

But to find it, you have to be willing to risk losing the kind of love that only survives inside silence.

That's the test:

It's not about being lovable, but loving yourself enough to tell the truth, even if it ends things.

That is the turning point.

That is when you stop trading parts of yourself just to be held.

That is when you realize: The love that couldn't hold your truth was never meant to hold you.

Love, Truth, and True Love

What Stays When the Silence is Gone

Love

It is the first thing we reach for. The first thing we fear losing.

It can be tender or overwhelming, healing or consuming.

We often think love alone is enough.

But in reality:

Love without truth becomes a beautiful lie.

Love can cling.

Love can beg.

Love can hold on to what no longer honors the soul.

Love can also keep you silent. Not out of cruelty, but out of fear, fear of hurting someone, fear of being alone, or fear of breaking what once felt perfect.

So, we hold on.

We perform.

We shrink.

And in doing so, we mistake closeness for connection. We mistake comfort for honesty.

We mistake attachment for alignment.

Truth

Truth arrives quietly, but it never leaves.

It may live in the background for years, silently waiting, while you keep denying it.

Truth says:

"This no longer fits."

"This is not who you are."

"This love requires you to disappear."

Truth is the moment when silence becomes too heavy.

It is the breath you take before saying something real, even if it changes everything.

Truth will never ask you to betray yourself.

And sometimes, that means walking away from a love that does.

True Love

True love is not just affection; it is recognition. It is a space where you are allowed to be whole. Where your truth is not a threat, but a bridge.

Where you are not loved in spite of your depth, change, or honesty, but because of it.

True love doesn't silence you.

It doesn't ask you to choose between yourself and the relationship.

It says:

"I want the real you, even if it's hard. Even if it means things must change. Even if it means I have to change, too."

True love can hurt.

It can end.

But it never demands your soul as a sacrifice.

Not all love is true love.

And not all truth is welcome in love.

But when love and truth walk together, you've found something holy.

Love speaks.

Truth stands.

And true love listens without fear.

Truth Feeling

The Knowing Before the Words

There is a moment when something clicks inside you.

A pause.

A breath.

A shift so small it might go unnoticed by others, but to you, it feels like everything just changed, everything just aligned.

That is what truth feels like.

It's not an opinion.

Not a conclusion.

Not a dramatic breakthrough. It's a quiet clarity.

It says:

"This is real."

"This is me."

"This is what I can no longer deny."

You don't have to explain it.

You don't even have to act on it right away. But once it arrives, you can't unknow it.

Truth Has a Sensation

It lives in the body. In the loosening of the shoulders. In the deep breath that finally reaches the belly. And in the tears that come when you name what you've carried in silence.

You feel it when:

You speak, and something inside you exhales.

You walk away from something, and your chest lifts.

You tell the truth and your whole body says yes, even if your mind is scared.

You've Felt It Before

You've known what wasn't right before you could prove it.

You've known who you loved before you had the words.

You've known when a place, a path, or a person was no longer yours, because the feelings shifted, even if nothing else had.

That's truth.

Not always loud. Not always logical. But always real.

Let It Guide You

The world will ask you for facts.

For reasons.

For consistency.

But the soul will only ask you for honesty.

And honesty often begins with the subtle feeling you once ignored, but now choose to trust.

Trust the feeling that stays after the story ends.

That's where your truth begins.

The Connection Between Truth and Feelings

How Emotion Becomes a Doorway to the Real Truth

Real truth doesn't always arrive in words.

It often comes first as a feeling.

A tightness in your chest.

A hesitation in your voice.

A sudden heaviness around someone you once trusted.

A lightness when you finally say what's real.

Before truth becomes a language, it is sensation. And if you learn to trust your feelings, you'll often discover they knew the truth long before your mind did.

Feelings Speak in a Language the Mind Tries to Translate

We often try to understand before we feel.

But sometimes, understanding only comes after the feeling has been fully allowed.

Your sadness may not give you reasons right away.

Your anger might not explain itself politely.

Your joy may surprise you in places that don't make sense.

But every feeling carries data.

Not the kind that you can measure, but the kind only you recognize.

The kind that rings in your body like a tuning fork when something is finally true.

Truth and Feelings Are Mirrors

If you want to know what's true for you, ask your feelings, not just your thoughts.

Ask:

"What do I feel when I say this out loud?"

"Where does this decision live in my body?"

"Do I feel lighter or tighter when I imagine staying silent?"

The mind can lie to protect you, but the body rarely does.

Your feelings will always try to pull you toward truth, even when that truth is inconvenient, uncomfortable, or unfamiliar.

Let Feeling Lead You Home

When you ignore your feelings, you drift away from yourself.

When you listen to them, you begin to remember.

Your truth is not something you have to invent.

It's already inside you, beneath the performance, beyond the fear.

Feelings are not distractions; they are invitations.

And when you answer them with honesty,

you don't just find clarity; you find belonging.

Truth in Understanding

The More You Understand, the Less You Pretend

Understanding is not just knowledge.

It is intimacy.

It is sitting with something long enough to stop judging them.
It is listening to them without needing to win.

It is looking inward and saying:

"I want to see what's real, not what I wish was true."

That is where truth begins.

In stillness.

In curiosity.

In the courage to ask:

"What is actually here?"

"What part of me have I not yet tried to understand?"

Understanding Reveals What Performance Hides

You cannot understand what you are still performing.

You cannot understand others if you are still trying to be liked.

You cannot understand yourself if you are only interested in what sounds good.

Understanding requires humility.

It's what happens when the ego steps aside and presence steps forward.

And when you stay long enough with a question, truth begins to rise, gently, steadily, and without being forced out.

Understanding makes space. Truth fills it.

Truth Grows in the Soil of Understanding

We often think truth is a sharp sword, something we use to cut through confusion.

But more often, truth is a garden.

It grows when we tend to the roots of things.

When we ask:

Where did this belief come from?

What part of me is still afraid?

What am I trying to protect by staying silent?

Understanding doesn't always give you answers, but it clears away what's false.

And in that clearing, truth can finally breathe.

You Don't Need All the Answers to Know What's True

Understanding doesn't mean you figure it all out.

It means you become honest enough to stop pretending you already have.

And in that softening, something powerful happens: You begin to trust your experience.

You begin to feel what's true, even before it makes sense.

You begin to know yourself, not as a performance, but as a whole being who no longer needs to hide.

Truth is not the end of understanding.

It is what understanding brings you back to.

Not a conclusion.

A coming home.

The Other Side of Silence

Wholeness. Integration. Return.

This isn't the end.

This is the part where you stop hiding.

The part where truth is no longer an idea but a way of being.

The part where you realize that you were never broken, only buried beneath what you were told to be true.

Living Whole

You Don't Have to Split Yourself to Belong Anymore

Wholeness isn't perfection.

It isn't having all the answers or always being certain.

Wholeness is what happens when you stop abandoning parts of yourself just to be accepted.

It is:

- Speaking when you once stayed silent.

- Resting when you once hustled for worth.
- Saying I don't know without shame.
- Letting your past be seen without needing to erase it.

Wholeness is when all the parts of you are finally invited to the table:

The one who doubted.

The one who feared.

The one who changed.

The one who tells the truth now.

You don't reject any of them. You hold them.

You understand them. You let them come home.

You Become a Living Truth

When you live wholly:

You no longer chase connection. You become connected.

You no longer wait for permission. You become authority.

You no longer hide behind belief. You become curious.

You no longer fear change. You walk with it.

You no longer bury your truth. You accept it.

This is the other side of silence.

It's not always loud. But it's honest. And it's yours.

Wholeness doesn't mean you never fall back into fear.

It means you know how to come back to yourself when you do.

You made it.

Not just to the end of this book, but through parts of yourself that were waiting to be seen.

Through the noise of belief. Through the shadow of fear.

Through the fire of change. Through the ache and clarity of truth.

And now, you're here.

On the other side of silence.

Where your voice is not a performance. It is a presence.

Where your feelings are not distractions. They are a compass.

Where you no longer shrink to fit. Or fake peace to avoid loss. Or chase belonging by abandoning yourself.

You are home now.

Not in perfection. But in wholeness.

And if nothing else, let this remain true:

You do not have to trade your truth for love.

You do not have to hide the parts of you that still shake.

You do not need to know everything before you begin again.

You only need to stay with yourself, honestly, gently, and with care.

That's what healing is. That's what return is.

That's what it means to unlearn the silence. Thank you for being brave enough to listen. Not just to these words, but to your own.

We are all just remembering who we were before the noise. And you, dear reader, are closer than you think.

A Quiet Return

What part of you is ready to speak again?

What truth have you been waiting to live?

What does your wholeness sound like now?

Don't rush the answers.

Let them rise slowly.

Truth doesn't shout. It waits.

And now you know how to listen.

When the Silence Was Gone

When the silence was gone,

I did not become someone new; I became someone real.

I stopped explaining what no longer made sense and started listening to the part of me that always did. I let the lie of being "too much" fall apart in my hands, and I cradled what remained: raw, radiant, whole.

It was never about finding answers, but about remembering that I was allowed to ask questions and still belong.

And when I finally told the truth, not to the world, but to myself, I found that I was still loved.

Still breathing.

Still here.

This is what it means to unlearn the silence:

To trust your own voice even if it trembles.

To be honest even if it costs you comfort.

To come home to yourself without asking permission.

And to know, finally, that this has always been enough.

For the Journey After

These reflections are invitations, not to fix yourself, but to ask yourself. Use them slowly. Softly. In your time.

1. Belief

What belief have I outgrown but still carry?

Whose voices shaped those beliefs?

What would I believe if I trusted my own experience?

2. Fear

What is fear trying to protect in me?

What am I afraid would happen if I told the full truth?

What might be possible beyond fear?

3. Change

What version of me is ready to end?

What change am I resisting because I think I'm not ready?

Where in my life is change already happening?

4. Truth

What truth have I been whispering to myself?

What does my body feel like when something is real?

Where do I no longer feel aligned?

5. Understanding

What parts of me have I silenced to fit in?

What does understanding look like in my everyday life?

What would it mean to live without performing?

And one final question to return to, again and again:

What is true for me now?

Because your truth will evolve, but your right to live it, never will.

Chapter Six:

Love and Light

You will be told to stay soft. You will be told to stay small. But your soul was not made to whisper.

There comes a moment in every inner journey when softness is no longer enough. When being kind to the world means finally being honest with yourself. When healing stops looking like hiding, and starts looking like rising.

This is that moment.

Not about pretending everything is love and light, but about becoming it.

Love and light are not decorations. They are decisions.

They are actions taken in the fire of transformation. They are boundaries drawn with sacred intention.

They are the truths spoken with clarity. Even when your voice trembles, say:

"I do not whisper love and light. I speak it like a truth that cannot be unlearned."

Love is not a soft surrender. It is a wild, conscious choice to stand tall with your heart open, even when the world tells you to fold.

It is the fire in your chest when you rise after breaking. The echo of your own name when you finally call yourself home.

And light?

Light is not just a comfort.

It is power. It is clarity. It is the refusal to remain in shadow when you were born to blaze.

They told you to dim. To be small.

To be sweet. To be silent.

But you were never made to shrink. You were made to see.

You were made to know.

You were made to burn through the illusion and stand in truth.

So let love be your weapon, not of war, but of liberation. Let it cut through fear. Let it melt the armor. Let it reach every version of you that thought you had to hide.

And let light be your voice.

Let it speak when silence becomes too heavy. Let it roar when truth is buried.

Let it lead, no matter how long you've wandered.

Love and light are not pretty words. It is a force. A revolution. A way of being that will shatter chains you forgot were holding you.

This is not the time to play small. This is the moment to rise.

In love. In light. In full.

You will forget sometimes, you will fall back into old patterns, you will soften when you should speak, and you will silence the roar within you. But each time, remember who you are, you return stronger. Not harder, but stronger.

Because love is your anchor, and light is your fire.

And together, they make you unshakable.

We Focus on the Massager and Forget the Message

We live in a world that craves comfort, longs for relief from the pain, seeks ease from pressure, and desires to escape from the chaos within.

So, when something soothes us, we cling to it. We trust the gentle hand, the calming words, the familiar rhythm of someone or something that makes us feel better.

And there's nothing wrong with comfort. We all need it. But sometimes, comfort becomes a distraction.

We pay attention to the massager, the person, the voice, the presence, and forget the message they carry.

We remember how we felt in the moment, but not what we were meant to hear.

The massager touches the tension in our backs, but the message touches the tension in our lives.

One releases the muscle. The other invites us to release the mask.

We want healing without disruption. Peace without truth.

A new life without the shedding of the old.

But real messages are not always soft. They don't always arrive in comfort.

Sometimes they come to unsettle, to stir, to break what no longer serves.

We idolize the guide and forget the guidance.

We praise the sermon and ignore the transformation it asks of us.

We quote the speaker and overlook the responsibility in the words.

The massager is not the healing; they are the vessel.

The message is the call.

It asks us to listen. To respond. To shift.

So, the next time we're drawn to a voice, a moment, or a feeling of relief, let us pause and ask:

What is the message here for me?

Not just how it made me feel, but what it's asking me to face, to change, or to become.

Comfort passes.

But the message, if heard, transforms.

Living in truth isn't only about what you say; it's about who you are when no one is watching.

Truth shows itself not just in words, but in the way we protect our dignity and live in integrity.

Truth is not just something we discover; it's something we choose to live.

Many people know the truth but walk in fear. Others speak the truth but live in contradiction.

To truly live in truth is to let it shape both how we see ourselves and how we act in the world.

That's where dignity and integrity come in, not as ideals, but as expressions of truth lived with courage.

Dignity and Integrity: The Soul's Backbone

There are things we're taught to chase: success, recognition, being liked, being right, the list goes on.

But, only a few are taught to protect their dignity or guard their integrity.

And yet, these two are the very backbone of a life lived in truth.

Dignity is not loud.

It's not something you wear to impress.

It's not dependent on applause or how many people approve of you.

Dignity is that quiet strength within you that says:

"I matter, not because of what I've done, but because I exist."

It's the knowing that even when your voice shakes, or when the world turns away, you don't lose yourself.

Dignity allows you to walk out of rooms where you're not respected and stay standing in moments that try to reduce you.

It is not arrogance.

It is not stubborn pride.

It is a recognition of your own sacred worth, a worth that no external voice can increase or decrease.

Dignity cannot be given. It must be owned.

Integrity is how you protect that worth in the world.

It is living in alignment with your values, your truth, your conscience, even when it costs you comfort or connection.

It is the refusal to say yes when your heart says no.

The courage to walk away when something violates your peace.

Integrity doesn't mean perfection; it means consistency.

It means you don't live in pieces, acting one way in private and another in public.

It is the commitment to being whole, even when being whole is inconvenient.

When you lie to yourself to be accepted, your integrity begins to leak.

When you betray what you know is right to stay safe, the soul aches.

Together, they are powerful.

Dignity says:

"I am worthy, whether you see it or not."

Integrity answers:

"And because I am worthy, I will not shrink, perform, or betray myself to be seen."

They are not tools to impress the world; they are foundations to stand on when the world forgets who you are.

A person who walks with both dignity and integrity cannot be easily manipulated.

They do not beg for validation.

They don't try to fit the moment; they shape the moment by simply being rooted in truth.

When you lose your way, come back to this:

Am I living in a way that honors my dignity?

Are my choices in integrity with what I know to be true?

That is the compass. Not applause.

Not an image. Not fear.

But the deep alignment between what you carry inside... and how you live it out.